KAILYN LOWRY

WITH ADRIENNE WENNER

PRIDE OVER PITY

A POST HILL PRESS BOOK

To everyone who taught me that life does not end at sixteen and pregnant. It is only the beginning.

A POST HILL PRESS BOOK
ISBN (trade paperback): 978-1-68261-284-2
ISBN (hardcover): 978-1-61868-979-5
ISBN (eBook): 978-1-61868-9-801

Pride Over Pity

Cover design by Travis Franklin
Interior design and typesetting by Neuwirth & Associates, Inc.

"Beauty is Sizeless" photography on page 122 by Kate Hedrick

Post Hill Press
posthillpress.com

MTV
1515 Broadway
New York, NY 10036
mtv.com

Published in the United States of America

This work is a memoir. It reflects the author's present recollections of her experiences over a period of years. Certain names, locations, and identifying characteristics have been changed. Dialogue and events have been recreated from memory, and, in some cases, have been compressed to convey the substance of what was said or what occurred.

The views and opinions in the book are solely those of the author and do not represent the views of MTV, its parent company, Viacom Inc., or the publisher, Post Hill Press.

CONTENTS

I felt different. There was something about me that just wasn't the same. I had to clear the mess up right now. I locked myself in the bathroom and peed on the little stick that would determine my fate. I stared at the strip as the little plastic window revealed a positive sign. I laughed nervously and threw it onto the bathroom counter. Pregnant? I was pregnant? But I was only 17. The reality of the situation took a while to sink in, but once I accepted that the test wasn't lying, I knew my life would never be the same again.

1

The Intoxicatingly Wicked Witch

My six-year-old legs were not long enough to help me run through the house fast enough. As I made a turn around the kitchen island, my heart pounded a little faster. Her dodgy movements were slow and predictable, but my fear never lessened.

"I'm gonna get you my pretty," my mom slurred in a high-pitched voice. She popped out from behind the kitchen island and cackled evilly, "And your little dog too!" The poor yet spooky imitation was enough to send me running out of the house, but I settled for screaming and sensibly locking myself in her bedroom.

My mom knew Mrs. Gulch, aka the Wicked Witch of the West, scared me more than anything. To have a fictional villain come to life is a child's worst nightmare, but for me this was typical for my mother during her escapades. At the time

I never understood why my mom always transformed into the bad witch after drinking. Nobody liked her. Nobody wanted to be her. As birthdays flew by, I realized the problem was much bigger than what it seemed. My mother was an alcoholic.

I didn't have anything to compare my family to, so I struggled to understand what was going on with her on my own. I began to question everything. Is it curable? How long had she been this way? Why her? Why me? Was I the only one who thought she had a serious problem? At such a young age, normal isn't yet defined, but I sensed my family was different. There was no hiding the fact that my father wasn't and hadn't been in the picture since I was a baby, but drinking was still something I did not fully understand—yet.

I guess the only part of my childhood that could be considered typical was my insatiable need to be active. Every bright-eyed child holds hopes and dreams closer than reality. In fact, at that age, dreams matter more than what reality or destiny hold in store for you. It's so beautiful to think that, at that age, I didn't believe anything could hold me back. Becoming president of the United States, starting my own clothing line, becoming a vet, a dentist, or maybe even a singer seemed like achievable goals back then. The future held endless possibilities—until it started to feel like my mother was a big deadbolt on the door. I don't recall her ever giving me outlets to test my dreams out on. I wasn't involved in clubs or sports or any sort of activity or hobby.

It seemed like my mother had enough trouble just remembering to pick me up from school. I remember being dropped off at friends' houses and sometimes not getting a phone call for what seemed like days. For most kids, sleeping over multiple nights in a row is a chance to have unsupervised fun. For me, it meant wondering when I would see my mom again. I didn't want to be part of the tumultuous lifestyle created by her unpredictable behavior. I wanted consistency and stability, but I felt like my childhood lacked structure and steady parenting. I found myself weaving into the crazy more without recognizing that it wasn't normal. I even started to lie to cover for my mother's behavior.

The day after September 11, 2001, my mother came to pick me up from my after-school program at Lakeside Elementary School. It was a program where the teachers sent you to an open space in the school—like the gym or cafeteria—until about 5:00 or 6:00 when your parents would pick you up on their way home from work.

The previous day had been marked in American history as one of tragedy and loss on our soil. Everyone can remember where they were and what they were doing when the planes crashed. The following day, there was a heavy silence around the school. Even though I was only in the fourth grade, I was aware of a sense of the atmosphere being off.

Sitting between the two tables at the front of the cafeteria, the pair of teachers in charge watched as my mom leaned over the sign out sheet. Their disparaging glances caused a sense of a panic to rise in my chest. I rushed up to my mom so she didn't have the chance to speak to them. Did Jack Daniels suddenly make a perfume? Every word pouring out of her mouth sounded slurred. I was embarrassed and hung my head in shame, hoping no one else caught on as fast as I did. I thought I had gotten away without being interrogated, but the next day my guidance counselor called me into his office.

"My cousin works in New York City so my mom was really shook up," the rehearsed line rolled off my tongue in a monotone.

"Is that really it, Kailyn?"

"Yes," I replied, "she was just really worried."

That was the day I started lying for my mother's alcoholism. In that moment, I became an adult. It became my natural instinct to take care of people because it felt like my mother couldn't take care of herself—or me. Cleaning up vomit after a hard night of drinking made me look a little like Cinderella, except my version was even more twisted than the Brothers Grimm could imagine up.

Although I was fortunate enough that my mom was able to provide clothing, a roof over my head, and food on the table, her job working at multiple bars as a bartender caused more problems than it was worth. I remember how sometimes, when she got off of work, she'd disappear for a few days. Meanwhile, the person she hired to watch over me was, unbeknownst to my mom, a coke-snorting babysitter—who preferred the dollar bill method. In those times, when she would disappear for days without warning, I'd wonder if I would ever see her again. The possibility of her becoming a newspaper headline seemed inevitable to me because of her impulsive lifestyle. I guess no one told her she wasn't a rock star.

I'd like to pretend my mom never hurt me, but the truth is she did. It felt like a bottle of liquid brought her more joy than spending time with her own daughter. There's no denying I took it personally. How could I not? At some point I gave up on her because it seemed like a disease and I knew that disease wasn't thinking of my mom's best interest or mine. The insatiable need would always win out over a desire to make our lives better.

In fourth grade I moved to the next town over and spent a solid two years there. I was nearly always alone unless my mom had paid the babysitter by way of cigarettes. I wasn't sure who I was becoming or what I wanted. The deadly combination of loneliness and no sense of self hadn't become lethal quite yet, but I was seriously sick of moving around. As I entered middle school we moved again, this time even further away to Whitehall.

Moving from rural Pennsylvania, where everyone knows you and your family, to a more populated area didn't help my social standing. Moving around so much took me away from the few friends I had and, if anything, I was more withdrawn than ever. No one understood my situation, which made everything even more difficult for me.

No matter how lonely and isolated I became, the moving didn't stop and neither did the boyfriends my mom was racking up. She wasn't happy with herself so I think she hitched herself to others to escape feeling that way. When I was a freshman, one of the boyfriends tried getting her help. She listened to him and signed temporary custody over to my neighbors, the Hopwoods. I lived with them for a couple of months, while she pulled herself together. The Hopwoods knew my mom had issues and were willing to take me on to alleviate the stress in hopes that my mom would use the opportunity to get the help she needed. As I remember it, while she was supposedly doing her part to get better, my mom moved out of the house without giving me a heads up. Along with her boyfriend, she picked up and left, leaving me to run wild and free.

Every time my mom got help I secretly held onto a little bit of hope that she might look for a new job or change her way of life. But in the end nothing ever changed because it seemed like she never truly wanted to get better. I think that she was afraid of change because it would have meant struggling for a higher standard of living. It's easier to crawl around on the ground than it is to stumble while trying to achieve full balance. I think my mom always chose crawling because she preferred comfort to working for a better life

I did too in a way. Without much adult supervision, I got away with anything I wanted to. I had too much pent up anger and too much freedom for a teenager. Smoking pot became the hobby I'd never had as a little girl. It made me feel like I was part of a group. But it didn't take away the hurt or fury I was holding onto. If anything, it contributed to my self-destruction.

Meanwhile, I was getting into fights at my high school. At first my defiance was mostly verbal. Anyone I disagreed with would get attitude from me. I talked back to teachers, peers, anyone who rubbed me the wrong way. Occasionally, I got physical and would throw a punch at the person bothering me. The consequences for my aggressive behavior began with in-school suspensions, but eventually I landed a ten-day out of school suspension. In retrospect, this acting out was an outlet for my anger and frustration. It also placed in me a particular group of friends the way smoking pot did.

By the end of my freshman year, the trouble I was getting into escalated to the point that there was no way I could pull a solid four years at that school, so I moved back to Nazareth with my mom and her boyfriend to start anew as a sophomore. My life felt a bit like the movie, *Thirteen.* I had started out as a good kid, but just like Evan Rachel Wood's character, I felt alone and angry and this led me to make very poor choices. Although I can't deny I sometimes enjoyed the lack of parental supervision, it was hard to be left alone. Children and Youth services came and went. They tried intervening, but with no proof of neglect, they had no jurisdiction. I had all the basics: food, clothing, and shelter.

TOP: Me, 1 year old. BOTTOM: Me, 3 years old.

It was hard for me feeling that my mother seemed to choose alcohol over me, but my sense has always been that she drank to mask the pain of losing her sister, Jodi, who was killed in a car accident when they were in high school. My mother has never really recovered from the loss.

She and Jodi were opposites. From what I can piece together, they had a sisterly rivalry. Representing the two spectrums as varsity cheerleaders, my mom was the partier and Jodi was the studious one who kept out of trouble. The night of my Aunt Jodi's death, they had gone out together, but eventually parted ways. At around round 11:00 p.m. word had begun to spread about a terrible car accident. My mom ran to the scene, fearing the worst.

Her memory of the event is slow, faded, and possibly factually incorrect. She remembers hundreds of bystanders looking on as her sister was placed in the ambulance. In reality, there weren't many people present at the scene of the accident. Maybe my mom imagined a crowd to feel like she was surrounded and not alone watching her sister being pulled from the wreckage of the accident. She was the one who made the phone call to my grandparents, informing them that Jodi had been in a serious accident. At the hospital, they learned Jodi was brain dead. My mom told me that my grandparents made the painful decision to pull her off of life support.

My Uncle Jerry, my mom's brother, believes that when someone dies all the bad is forgotten about that person. Maybe the large lurking shadow my mother seems to always be running from is Jodi's memory. No matter what my mom does, she can never live up to the memory of the "good" sister who died so tragically.

The demons that had consumed my mother were now doing permanent damage to my well-being. As I settled into my new high school, our bad habits followed us. The freedom to go where I pleased resulted in me smoking constantly, more than ever before. Smoking weed had become my escape from loneliness.

2

SIDEWALK SEX

If I ever gaze at the past, I shudder. I shudder to count how many times I mistakenly thought I was loved. I quiver unpleasantly to recall the person I used to be and how I acted in some of my relationships. Looking back, it's not surprising that I turned to boys for love so early. I needed appreciation. I needed to feel worthy. Most of all I needed support.

I had my first boyfriend in eighth grade, nothing serious but very exciting. He turned my cheeks red and made me giggle. I became a silly little girl around him. We were only dating for a few months, but because some of my girlfriends were sexually active I felt pressured into wanting to get rid of my virginity, too.

A year before that, I barely knew what sex was. Now, suddenly, here I was pushing my boyfriend to do what we had just learned not to do in sex education. If *Mean Girls* had come out a little earlier I would have learned, "Don't have sex because you will get pregnant and die." Honestly, that might have been enough to scare my naïve self. But as it was, the little knowledge I had just made me curious and experimental, not frightened.

My inexperience shone brighter than the sun that spring. The April weather was still a little shaky, just warm enough to allow teens and wildlife to come out from hibernation. There are very few stimulating events in rural Pennsylvania, so we did what most bored teenagers do—got into trouble in our pursuit of something remotely interesting to do.

As young kids, we had no cars or empty apartments to have privacy in, so we pretty much hung out on the streets of our neighborhood. One night, as my friends rounded the corner, my boyfriend and I hung back. The concrete sidewalk had no summer warmth. It was a cold reminder that we were still a couple months shy of sun bathing. Suddenly, my pants and underwear were pulled down while my shirt stayed on. Our movements and his touch were unromantic. What should have been natural felt stiff. The instinctual was off. The worst part was my friends knew what we were up to.

The sun seemed to set and rise in my head, when in reality the big moment was over in a couple of minutes. Why does losing your virginity have to be so weird? I barely had any inclination then as to why, but in retrospect it is so obvious. I was too young to understand that I wasn't ready—physically or emotionally—for sex. I believed then that I had to have sex to keep up with my friends, so I just wanted to get the embarrassing virgin sticker off my forehead. Now, I wish I hadn't ripped it off so quickly. Virginity isn't a Band-aid.

There's no wound. In fact, as a virgin you're unscathed in those terms.

Once it was over, I was relieved to cover myself up and run home, blood trickling down my leg. Sex education didn't warn us girls about all the blood. They should have been clearer. I wasn't expecting a second monthly gift from Mother Nature, yet it sure seemed like she was being extra generous. Either that or *Mean Girls* was right: I was dying.

I didn't feel any humiliation because there was no one at home to question my appearance. The lights were out, so I changed out of the evidence in darkness. Now that it was over, I was relieved. I was actually comforted by the thought that I was somehow a "new" girl. In the end, my first boyfriend and I were together for a year, which is a lifetime if you're in the eighth grade. The few more times we had sex, it was still awkward and strange. The extremely uncomfortable nature of these experiences convinced me that this kind of intimacy should be reserved for long-term relationships only. However, although I wish I had reserved my first time for someone very special, I refuse to regret something I can't change now.

♦

In ninth grade I started seeing Toby. Although I would definitely put him into the long-term boyfriend category, during the two years that we were on-again-off-again, sex wasn't a part of our relationship. He was a typical popular guy who everyone wanted to be friends with, except that he also had a whirlwind of issues because his mother and father had recently split up. The anger was justified in every way, but I was in no place to be someone else's therapist—I needed one of my own.

Being asked to sleep over a guy's house is usually unsubtle code for sleeping together, but Toby was usually more straightforward so I didn't initially feel too pressured when he asked me to stay over at his house one night. As soon as I arrived, his friend started making fun of him about us not having sex. The dumb peer pressure pissed me off and their typical boy banter made me feel less close to Toby as the night wore on. Still, I was thankful for his friend's irritating presence because Toby's parents were out and I didn't want him to believe we'd take advantage of that to have sex. Unfortunately, his friend ended up leaving so we went to bed. He took me by the hand and led me up to a room upstairs. He pleaded his case and I quickly denied him.

"Let's have a baby so we can stay together forever."

The idea was absurd but Toby wouldn't take no for an answer. Everything about that night is a haze besides his proposition. Mostly I remember the sensory details. It went from being a dark room to me feeling just as pitch black as the environment. I didn't want to sleep with Toby, but he persisted. Denying him seemed fruitless. I believed Toby loved me so I decided I could give him this one thing as long as he wore a condom. He obliged my one request, yet something was off—literally.

"Where's the condom?" I questioned him when it was over.

"I took it off." The four words caused my heart to stop flittering for a moment. Off? He took it off?

"WHY did you take it off?"

Most guys would be freaking out, but his shrug was careless.

I should have been furious, but I was too terrified and consumed with worry. After that, Toby ignored all my attempts to communicate with him. I had never felt so down on myself, ever. Why was he shutting me out? I don't know why he thought getting me pregnant would be the answer to his problems (especially since he wouldn't talk to me) but to my dismay, his wish came true.

I took my first pregnancy test at fifteen in a Walmart bathroom. The little money scraped up from coins and random bills could have been enough to pay for a cute shirt I had been eyeing up at the mall, but instead it bought me a pregnancy test that offered a blurry picture of my future—a high school dropout, buried under piles of dirty diapers.

The only person I had to turn to was the one person I did not want to tell. My mom needed to know, though. Unfortunately, she seemed less concerned for my future than she was for her reputation. I think she felt that if she became a knocked up teen, she'd be looked at as a failure. She was adamant that I would not be allowed to deliver this baby into the world, even though deep down that was what I wanted. I remember my mother was so proactive about preventing my pregnancy from going any further that she sought out Toby's family to demand money to pay for the abortion. She threatened to press charges, which she knew meant he would lose his shot at a college scholarship. His family had no choice unless they wanted their son to be ruined.

Our parents made us attend abortion counseling sessions at a local clinic, where we were required to watch informative videos and to speak with a counselor. Between my mom and the counselor, my choices seemed limited. I remember my mom saying that I wouldn't be able to live with her and asking where I was planning to live. Those words from my mom impacted me just as hard as the videos did. It made me feel like I would be kicked out of the house and that my family would turn against me. The counselors reminded me that I was sixteen and I didn't have a car, a job, or even a license.

The next step proved to be as disturbing to me as the counseling sessions. Toby's dad and my mom picked a discreet location. We met at a Wawa—one I can't even drive by anymore without having an anxiety attack—to make the exchange. I had overheard my mom say to a friend that she might ask for more money than what the abortion cost. Was she trying to profit from the unfortunate situation? Watching through the window of my mom's car, I witnessed their stoic expressions as they made the no nonsense handover. The exchange looked a bit like a poorly planned drug deal in broad daylight. That was it. The money would pay for the abortion to terminate my baby.

My mom tried to confuse the situation by telling me that I had been RAPED. Rape is such a scary subject. What exactly constitutes rape? It's such a muddy word. Abortion is even darker, although less murky. The two together turned my heart to palpitations. These scary words belonged to an adult world that at the time meant little to me because I thought Toby loved me. How childish I was. I was so naïve that I had no idea how grave a situation I was in. I cared more about Toby loving me than my own well-being. But it was beginning to dawn on me that maybe his "love" wasn't good for me.

♦

On a birthday that should be remembered fondly, my happiness wasn't the priority or theme of the day. The sixteenth birthday bash I threw in my head had cake, friends, and many jokes of how everyone should watch the road for my crazy driving. I wanted to be at the DMV getting the permit that would give me freedom from the hell I sometimes lived in.

I wanted to be opening a few presents, hoping for clothing. But there was no joyful celebration for me that day. There were no gifts to receive, only one to be taken.

While I was marking my sixteenth year on earth, a precious life was being snuffed out before it even began. I didn't feel like blowing out candles to wish for the hopeless miracles of my mom never drinking again or my father appearing out of thin air. The only reasonable birthday wish for me was a giant memory eraser because I spent my sixteenth birthday in a clinic.

I wasn't alone. Toby's parents forced him to sit through the entire procedure with me. I was thankful he was present but he didn't need to be. My mind was too busy fighting against the truth to even notice he was there. Unfortunately, my mother was right: I was not capable of taking care of a child. The emptiness was total. I swear they didn't just suck out my uterus. It felt as though they had taken every little fiber of my being. When it was done, there was no baby. It was like he or she had never existed. I was expected to forget about the fetus. I could look to science for comfort that the genderless little squiggle was never a human being, but the truth was I felt a mother's grief. I didn't want to let go.

I had lost everything, but Toby still had what mattered to him. He had scholarships ready to send him off to a great future. I was the one who had to endure the pain and overcome the damage. On top of all that broken glass, my reputation at school was ruined.

Having an abortion and feeling like you have been raped isn't ever over. The experience added a weight to my feet, a few extra hundred pounds to the already heavy stack I was dragging around. With this heavy baggage, I had to walk into a new school. I had to meet new people. I knew I would have to date again. I would have to shelter this horrible secret in order not to be judged. At sixteen I was leaving black stains wherever I went.

3

My Precious Prom Night

The first time we met was at a McDonald's. I don't know if it was the romantic red and yellow decor that set the tone of the evening. Or maybe the aroma of potatoes and chicken frying in scalding hot oil was an aphrodisiac. McDonald's isn't exactly the classiest place you can meet a significant other, but I guess I could give myself half a point for not meeting him at a dive bar where contracting hepatitis is a given.

The experience was underwhelming. I wasn't impressed by him. I wasn't instantly attracted. No sparks even ignited, let alone flew. First impressions truly mean very little. Initially, Jo seemed weird to me. He was so different from the cocky boys I was used to. His quietness wasn't awkward, more mysterious and alluring. Things between us began so low key,

I never would have guessed we were destined to be a part of one another's lives forever. How was I supposed to know meeting this weird kid was fate?

When we first met, I had no intention of pursuing Jo. I probably wouldn't have even seen him ever again if it weren't for a mutual friend who had a crush on me. In the beginning, the three of us hung out together. This provided a neutral ground for Jo and me to start on, and our friendship progressed slowly over time. We didn't rush into a relationship or anything sexual, but gradually I developed a crush on him and what had started out as group outings began to turn more intimate.

The first time Jo invited me over to his house I was stunned by what a contradiction he was. He wore baggy clothes and brands that made him look like a hood kid, but it turned out he lived in a six-bedroom house complete with nice cars. He had a close-knit family, who worked incredibly hard for what they had. It seemed odd to me that he would try so hard to represent a different lifestyle than what he lived, but despite all that I liked Jo. He seemed like a genuinely good guy compared to most that I had encountered.

Our first "date" felt like it was broadcast to the nation. Even though it was just our families, that was plenty of eyes for us. Since I didn't have my license yet, I had my mom drop me off and pick me up. Even just watching a movie at Jo's house held a bit of pressure because both our families knew we were becoming a couple—or so I thought.

The bump in the road appeared when Jo asked to have sex with me before we were official. Because of my past experiences, I assumed Jo was a typical guy who wanted nothing more than sex—no matter how he got it. Did I have the word "tramp" tattooed on my forehead? I had sworn to myself that I would never have sex again outside of a solid relationship. I had already been through so much between the abortion and my relationship with Toby. I didn't want to be caught in a sleazy trap where I was being used for sex, so I refused Jo.

Jo didn't push me after I said point blank I wasn't ready for sex. After that, he did me justice by showing commitment and asking me out officially. It was the old "Do you wanna be my girl?" How I fell so hard for that line is beyond me. Instead of listening to my instincts, I allowed him to reel me in because I realized I had judged him too quickly.

♦

From the beginning, there were little glimpses of what we were heading to. Our so-called honeymoon period lasted shorter than the time it takes to say those words. I guess we never really got off to a healthy start. We broke up every other week for various reasons. His parents didn't want him to date me because his grades were dropping. Our personalities clashed and, on top of all our fighting, there was the most obvious truth: it's hard to be in a young relationship. I don't know why or how our relationship lasted, but through thick and thin our bumpy path continued right up until May of Jo's senior year (my junior year). By then, we had officially been together for nearly nine months. Every high school senior knows what May is for: graduation and prom. These are the celebrations that mark the end of high school, but prom never meant much to me. This Cinderella's expectations of the ball were very low. I figured it would be like any other school dance—grinding, drama, and maybe a couple fights. The only difference was I'd be witnessing it all clad in a gown.

Me and Jo, getting ready for prom.

Easily, the pampering was the best part. Like a true princess, I had my nails and hair done by my mother's best friend. My prom dress was from New York City, so compared to the other girls' low-key dresses I felt like royalty. The dress was the best part of a truly amazing birthday present from my cousins Jen and Candy, who are the closest I've ever had to siblings. They have always been heavily involved in my life, babysitting for me whenever possible and visiting every holiday after they both went away for college. Earlier that year they had given me a trip to New York as a birthday present. They paid for the bus ticket, showed me around the city, and took me to a Broadway show. For fun we had ventured into stores to look at prom dresses. I ended up falling in love with one in particular and they bought it for me as a gift. They were my fairy godmothers.

Feeling beautiful, I headed out for the night, but first I made a quick stop at a cousin's baby shower, dressed in full prom attire. I didn't realize it at the time, but it was as if the universe was warning me that my life as a carefree teen was about to end because May 16th, 2009 turned out to be a very important date in my life—one that had nothing to do with prom.

Stopped at my cousin's baby shower on the way to prom, the night Isaac was conceived.

Posing for prom.

The entire night seemed geared towards anything but dancing. There were groups grinding against one another everywhere you looked. A couple of boys were conspicuously huddled in a corner, taking swallows out of a flask. Teachers were scrambling to cut through any open space in order to break up lip-locked couples. Drama surfaced through the cracks of each mini event, spreading from the dance floor to the tables.

The classic teenage night of debauchery pushed on through rap, electronic dance music, and the out of place Blink 182 song. The music created a joyful atmosphere. All of my friends were present, happier than ever. Even Jo and I were taking a break from fighting for a little while to just enjoy ourselves. We owed it to our rocky relationship. We may not have been a typical happy couple, but that night we felt like we could almost be normal for a change.

The mini dream ended when the speakers blew out and hundreds of Easton High School students were left bummed and stranded. This abrupt early ending to the dance pushed the after-prom activities up on the schedule. Trouble was coming to get most prom attendees, and Jo and I were no exception. We drove to a deserted location, where the only eyes belonged to rundown buildings that hadn't seen the light of day for ages. The pouring down rain tapped heavily on the car as our clothes peeled off. The zipper on my dress fell quicker than the rain outside.

I was not comfortable in the car. We were very close to Jo's house and just knowing that psyched me out. My mind raced with questions and worries. I was close with Jo's family. Janet, Jo's mom, had always impressed upon me that I could count on her if need be. Would I be betraying that bond by having sex with her son? Although the atmosphere wasn't really dead-on perfect, I felt in my heart Jo was the right person to be having sex with. My gut told me so. There was no comparing this feeling to sidewalk sex or sex I had been forced into. I loved Jo. And Jo loved me. We loved each other—fights and all.

Jo thought he was just losing his virginity that night. I thought I was finally having sex with someone who truly cared about me. Nope. Turned out we were making a baby.

4

16 . . . 17 AND PREGNANT

A woman's body doesn't lie. Mine knew right away. My period wasn't supposed to come for another week or so, but I had a feeling this time the monthly reminder wasn't on its way. This gut feeling overtook my head and I knew I had to take the test to be a hundred percent positive.

Buying a pregnancy test isn't as easy as you would think. There are different brands and some of them are expensive. All those commercials I had seen over the years should have been clicking in my head, but I was so terrified even the simple act of choosing which brand to buy was overwhelming. I didn't want to think about the last time I had to buy a pregnancy test. Like any protection mechanism, I had wiped the memory from my mind because the truth was too sad to confront. But now that I found myself having to buy another pregnancy test, the horrification I felt doubled when I really put the two together.

The circumstance I was in was so humiliating. I felt a whirlwind of stress and confusion. As I approached the counter, the repetition of events slid across my heavy, pounding heart. The stress of purchasing a pregnancy test and then taking it was so overwhelming that most of the details have been scratched from my brain. All I remember is that somehow I was able to pull myself together to get back home, where I locked the bathroom door, even though I was alone, and peed on the stick. Sounds sort of ridiculous, but it was nowhere near as comical as the scene in *Juno* where she drinks those jugs of Sunny D. I didn't really need fake juice to provide the test with what it needed, not when I was nervous beyond belief.

While I waited, I tried not to overanalyze the what-ifs. If I were pregnant, then I would deal. If not, then I had learned a very important lesson: use multiple methods of birth control. I was on the pill, but I hadn't always taken it properly and now I was learning the hard way that it had made it less effective.

The seconds passed by slowly. Finally, I picked up the plastic device and saw the plus sign. I laughed anxiously and threw it down onto the sink. How was this real life? I was pregnant? What was I going to do? I was seventeen. Seventeen-year-olds barely know how to take care of themselves. How would I support a baby? Would my mom force me into another abortion? I didn't want her to coerce Jo's parents into paying for the abortion. What was going to happen this time around?

I called my friend Marisa and asked her to come over. I didn't want to be alone in this state of frenzy. The room was no longer a solid box, but a blurred swirl around me. The words we exchanged held no thought or meaning because I couldn't function properly. I was too young for all of this to be happening to me AGAIN and now I had to live with the consequences of my mistake. But amidst all the confusion, there was one concrete idea I firmly probed.

"What if I don't want to be with Jo forever?"I asked, scared.

The question echoed in my head. I was too young to determine the course of the rest of my life, yet this baby growing inside of me couldn't wait for me to grow up. Maybe I wouldn't have to be with Jo forever, but if I was allowed to keep this baby (which I already knew in my heart was what I wanted) it surely meant he would always be a part of my life as my baby's father.

The chaotic conversation that was really just a bunch of repetitive questions and no answers came to a halt once I finally accepted I was really pregnant. Talking was useless and would get me nowhere until I dialed Jo's number. I didn't say much on the phone. I just told Jo he needed to come over as soon as possible. I spent the next fifteen minutes debating how to break the news gently. No seventeen-year-old boy wants to hear his girlfriend say, "I'm pregnant." When Jo finally arrived, he parked outside of my place and I went out to meet him.Every step and every movement to his car felt like the biggest moments of my existence. I couldn't bring myself to say those hauntingly life altering words, so I just handed him the white stick that represented our future.

Jo stared at the pregnancy test silently, freaking me out even more. I needed him to be responsive and comforting. He was the only person who had the ability to reassure me, but Jo didn't utter a single syllable. I couldn't tell if it had any impact on him whatsoever, so I got out of the car, possibly even more upset than I was before. If he wasn't on board,

I didn't know what kind of choices I would have. Abortion? Adoption? Raising a child on my own? Abortion is such a horrible word. Sadly, I knew exactly what it meant. The experience had been so horrific for me that I couldn't really bear to consider it as an option again. Once was almost impossible to recover from, twice would mean falling into a deep depression and never bobbing back up for air.

The next couple of weeks were an adjustment to say the least. After I told Jo he went home and told his mother, so his parents became aware almost immediately. Jo has a great, supportive family who will stand by him through any storm. They were the first people who sat us down to have a real solid talk about our future and the baby.

Janet, Jo's mother, had experience dealing with teen pregnancy considering she was once a teen mom herself. She had Eddie Jr., Jo's oldest brother, when she was sixteen and knew firsthand what we were going through and what we would be facing. She reiterated the same harsh facts I had heard in the abortion clinic. I understood the mountain we had to climb was sizable. This wasn't the first time I was hearing about the hardships of motherhood for a sixteen-year-old girl. *You're still in school. How are you going to afford it? It's so expensive. The diapers, the formula, the clothes they always grow out of, and not to mention the childcare you'll need all the time.*

Honestly, all those questions did terrify me, but in that moment I realized that I wasn't concerned with how other people would feel about whatever decision I made. Any link between abortion and my baby, even just the suggestion, made me squirm inside. I realized that this time it was not the solution for me. I knew now for sure abortion was absolutely off the table. I told Jo how I felt and he seemed to be on board.

We spoke with Jo's father about our decision. Since my home wasn't exactly the best environment in which to raise a baby, he promised to finish remodeling their basement to ensure we would have enough room and privacy for when the baby arrived. He explained to Jo that he would have to pay child support for eighteen years, if our relationship didn't work out, and then there would be college expenses. His parents impressed upon us the seriousness of our situation and how trying the next few months would be, let alone the next few years. I believe Jo felt forced to make an effort in our relationship.

Once this decision was made, it was time to let the secret out to the rest of Jo's family. He made an official announcement at his graduation party in front of his entire family. I was uncomfortable knowing Jo's big occasion was about to be overshadowed by this news we had. The quiet, reserved silence should have been because of a speech from his parents about his future and how proud they were of him. Instead Jo was announcing that I was pregnant. To my surprise, congratulations echoed from every corner of the room. His family's genuine support lifted my heart out of the pit of my stomach. Although I was convinced I was doing the right thing, their support made me feel so much more confident I could actually have this baby. We didn't receive any disapproval, just fair warnings of how challenging things would be. Everyone in his family made it known to me that, if I needed anything, they would be there for me. Their blessings meant the world to me. I needed to know others believed Jo and I were capable of succeeding and beating the odds.

We weren't alone. This little bit of relief removed a few of the weights I carried in the pit of my stomach, especially because his parents weren't setting deadlines or making ridiculous demands we could never meet. As long as Jo stayed in college, they promised to help us as much as possible. The stress and anxiety had already begun, but I knew I wasn't by myself. I was on the right road to making the best out of what we had. And as far as I was concerned, that road did not include my mother.

♦

I believed that the longer I withheld the news from my mother, the better off I'd be. It wasn't that I was afraid of her reaction; it was more that I was wary of the fights I'd have to put up with. There had already been enough yelling to last me a decade. I didn't need any more thrown into the mix. There was also a part of me that was trying to protect myself from more disappointment. I didn't believe that my mom was capable of stepping up and being my parent, even though I desperately needed her to be.

Months went by and the morning sickness I dreaded started up and didn't stop. Summer with its high heat and humidity is not a comfortable time for me as it is. Now, the changes to my body and the constant nausea only made it that much worse. While all of my friends were out in their bikinis, showing off their fast metabolisms and naturally thin bodies, I went into hiding. I couldn't wear a bikini or risk betraying my secret. I was only a few months into my pregnancy, but I was still worried I would be judged.

As summer drew to an end, I was ecstatic that the humidity was starting to wear off and layering clothing would be considered normal again. But the end of summer brought new problems that I had to face. Just like every other high school student, I wasn't exactly looking forward to returning to school, but this year I had a legitimate reason to dread the fluorescent-lit, generically decorated rooms. Sure, I could hide the pregnancy for a while, but soon I would be stared at and talked about down the hallways. It *was* high school, after all.

Meanwhile, I was so caught up worrying about how I would deal with the idle gossip at school, I almost forgot that I still had to come up with a plan to casually drop the news of my pregnancy on my mom. Based on the way she handled my last pregnancy, I didn't trust her to be supportive. I had decided to clue her in at the last minute because I felt like she didn't deserve to be involved. Having a child so young was going to be hard enough; I didn't need her slurring her opinion to me. However, that strategy went awry.

My body was plotting against me and it was becoming harder and harder to pretend that nothing had changed. My mom drove me to school a few times and nearly every time I needed her to pull over so I could vomit. I don't know if at first she conjured up some insane stomach flu that only hit in the morning to make sense of that, but eventually someone dished the news to her. In an ideal world, this would have been the moment my mom turned her life around for her future grandchild.

Oh, Kailyn! This wouldn't have happened if I had just paid attention to you! If I just would have been a better mother. This is all my fault.

Deep down I hoped that my mom would take on the persona of the concerned parent, unfortunately that's not what happened.

Cramped in the small kitchen of our tiny apartment, Janet, Jo's mother sat down at the table. The hesitant looks I shared with Jo betrayed the supposed secret we were about to unleash on my mother, who seemed to be in the know anyway. Janet had never been inside our apartment, another indicator to my mom this wasn't a happy talk. My mom had the audacity to sit there and cry after we told her. I was so infuriated I lost sight of any words thrown around. As alone as I had been, I still wanted guidance and a comforting hand on my back. All I got were her tears and I felt she had no right to cry.

5

I WANT MY MTV

My mom and I were forced to live amicably as mother and daughter while Jo's parents prepared the basement for us to move into. The awkwardness between us progressed as the pregnancy did, so I tried to find a distraction to take me away from how bad my living situation had become. MTV's huge new reality series, *16 and Pregnant*, had aired to a wide audience, including myself. Really, for me there couldn't have been anything more relatable on television. Reruns of *Boy Meets World* were always great, but this new MTV show had an emotional tug.

Most shows worth watching are controversial and *16 and Pregnant* was no exception. I understood the taboo idea behind it all but didn't care. The issue they were portraying was real. I was going through exactly the same things these girls were going through and I knew it was an important show that could help girls like me.

As *16 and Pregnant* gave me people to relate to, I became more interested in the show itself. Since I was becoming so emotionally invested, I decided to go on MTV's site to see if I could find more details. Crazy enough, MTV was casting for another season. I didn't think there would be any harm in applying. I was sure there would be so many applicants that my chances would be very low. I didn't give much thought to what would happen if I were chosen.

Two weeks later I was at Jo's house and my cell phone rang. It was a long distance number. Who could be calling me? I picked up on the off chance it was important. To my complete surprise, a casting agent was on the line and she explained she was calling on MTV's behalf. I talked to her for a little bit to discuss my current situation and the pregnancy. The phone call was very to the point. She basically just wanted to confirm my story. As we talked, I thought about what it would mean if I was chosen, but I didn't have any emotions about it just yet. I was convinced that the opportunity would probably fall through. This especially felt true as she explained the next step of the process, which was to fill out a questionnaire and send in home videos.

I interviewed my best friend, Jo, and my mom on camera. I wasn't positive Jo or my mom would agree to even do the interviews, but once I had them on board, there was only one last step to be considered for the show: film myself talking about my situation. I spoke about how I found out I was pregnant, what we were doing to move forward, and how my friends and family felt about all of it. Although it was the last thing I expected to happen, a few weeks later, I was signing paperwork and getting parental approval.

It was official. MTV had selected me to be part of the new hit show. But I had no idea what to expect. I felt strongly that it would be a great way to get my story out and hopefully inspire other girls to make good decisions, but I was too busy preparing for the baby I was about to have to really wrap my head around what being filmed for a television show would entail. At this point, I was still living at home with my mom, but by the time the cameras showed up she had agreed to sign custody over to Jo's parents and I had moved in with them. I was so preoccupied with the move and dealing with being pregnant that I barely gave the idea a second thought until the day the MTV crew showed up for the first day of filming. By that point I was nearly six months pregnant and showing. Of course, the first shot they wanted to take was at the one place I felt most uncomfortable—my high school.

At Nazareth High, I was the new girl and always would be because it was such a small community. All the other kids had grown up with one another through elementary and middle school and I had just jumped into Nazareth High School like an out of place character. Now this character had cameras following her around. Granted, I had signed up for all of it, but I wasn't prepared for the reactions. Even without the camera, the stares were enough for me to feel like I was under a microscope. I hoped the strangeness of it all would eventually begin to feel normal.

The first few hours of filming were the most awkward. I wasn't used to having a lot of attention directed at me and now I suddenly had cameras following me around, filming my every move. The impact on my life of being part of a reality television show was overwhelming and I wasn't sure if I could handle it.

PRIDE OVER PITY

TV is supposed to be glamorous, but real life isn't, especially when raging hormones affect all of your actions. The cameras caught me making irrational, emotional decisions that didn't really portray me at my best. And I wasn't the only one. Jo quickly became annoyed with the cameras and we fought more and more as my due date neared. The filming certainly wasn't helping our relationship. Jo knew just as well as I did the characters we were about to project on national television were not going to show us at our best, but the fact of the matter is we were being real and not holding back.

6

THE DREADED "D"

My life falls a tad bit short of a fairy tale, even though some days it does feel like there's as much drama as the movies. Like Lindsay Lohan in the *Parent Trap,* I had questions. What kind of job did my father have? Did he have other children? Most importantly, who was he? The dreaded "D" word was either avoided or pulverized like a piece of meat by my mother. I don't remember her ever having a single positive thing to say about him.

My dad disappeared from my life when I was six months old and to this day I have no idea what really happened between my parents. All I ever had was my mother's story, but judging from my own experience, my mother isn't exactly the easiest person to get along with. I knew there would be no magical explanation as to why my dad wasn't around, but I still felt like I needed answers.

My first few months on earth weren't normal by any stretch. From what I've been told, I was a very sick baby, run down by pneumonia. Instead of taking me to the doctor as was planned, my mother says that my dad whisked me away from Pennsylvania to Texas to raise me on his own. He did take me to the hospital once we arrived, but my mother came after him with detectives and lawyers and eventually got me back. Although my mom claimed that it was his controlling nature that led him to that plan of action, knowing that he had at least attempted to raise me on his own made me believe that my father was more than just a deadbeat dad. I wasn't satisfied with the story I was told because none of it explained why he wasn't involved in my life now.

I needed to know why.

What bothered me the most was that it just seemed like, to my dad, losing the custody battle had been grounds for giving up on me altogether. There was no restraining order keeping him from visiting me or at least sending a cheesy Hallmark card on my birthdays, yet from that moment on he had disappeared from my life. He didn't seem to care if I was doing okay. He didn't seem to care that I needed him in my life. The wounds were wide, open, and raw.

Then one random day, as I logged onto my Facebook page, I was unexpectedly given the opportunity to find the answers I had been looking for my whole life. There was a message from an unfamiliar name and no picture to help identify whom it could be. I read the message over and over. "You don't have to respond . . ." The words didn't seem desperate for my attention, but apparently my father's sister, Beth, had been searching for me on MySpace and other social networking sites for years. I felt inclined to know more about her and where she had been my whole life, so I responded.

As soon as I learned who she was and that she was connected to my mysterious father, I began fantasizing how my life would change for the better because I had always secretly hoped that one day he would come back to rescue me from my miserable life.

Me and my Aunt Beth.

The only problem with that fantasy was that I was now three months pregnant. Although I had always felt let down by my father for never being around, now I worried that *I* was the one who would be a disappointment to *him.* If he found out I was pregnant, would he still want to know me? Why would anyone want to enter my life at such a hectic, crazy time?

Turned out I didn't have to worry. Facebook messages turned into hours of phone conversations with my aunt and father, all of which were positive. My aunt invited me to visit her and her daughters in Texas. My father lived in Waco, a town outside Dallas, and since I would be in the immediate area already, I knew I wanted to include meeting him in this trip. It was a hundred percent my decision and my plan. I packed for a few days, minus the single precaution I received from my mom—hold no expectations. I thought I knew better than to trust her words of wisdom.

Granted, it was my Aunt Beth who had originally reached out to me and invited me to visit, but I wanted to believe my father was just as enthusiastic and if she hadn't invited me first, he would have eventually. Plus, after waiting so long, what harm could meeting him do? I didn't believe there was any way he could damage me any more than I had already been damaged. I thought my mother was just being negative, so I left her advice in Pennsylvania where I felt it belonged, and boarded a plane to Dallas, Texas. I was finally going to meet my father—Raymond.

We were in the thick of filming for *16 and Pregnant* and MTV wanted to capture this momentous moment in my life, so I agreed to let the cameras come along. It was actually very reassuring to have the MTV crew with me because it felt like they were a protective backup team, ready to swat my dad away if things went awry. Sifting through the crowd at the airport, I had an image in my head of a strong, tall man who would appear nervous and uneasy but still confident and strong. Instead, the man who greeted me had a mullet, missing teeth, and was at least a foot shorter than I thought he would be. Only the Texan twang proved to be intact.

Daddy. Dad. The old man. My father.

I wasn't expecting my dad to be sporting a cape and saving the world during his free time, but I had thought he'd seem a little more put together. Nothing about the man I was meeting now seemed consistent with what he had told me about himself. Really, he seemed to me like a mess of contradictions. Supposedly, he held two associate's degrees, yet I don't know if he had a job. He used to be a Marine and a bull rider, but he was absolutely out of shape with no trace of his former military self. It seemed to me that he had let himself go to the point of no return. I was supposed to be proud to call this man, Dad? He had told me he lived in a cozy two bedroom house, but the home he brought me to turned out to be a little shack. When he had described the quaintness of his place, I had pictured a cozy, little ranch. I was disappointed because I had expected to see my dad living comfortably. It felt like he was just coasting by, not living to the fullest. It seemed like he didn't care to make himself or any part of his life better. He was just settling.

I went to sleep that night, hoping that I would see things in a more positive light in the morning. Unfortunately, things went downhill from there. The next morning's Dunkin Donuts run should have been a decently cheap breakfast that he could treat me to, but when my dad asked me to borrow a twenty, I realized *I* was buying. Bumming money off of me, his pregnant teenage daughter, was the last straw in the haystack for me. Sure, he paid me back but it was yet another reminder that he was not the man I thought he would be.

My father seemed to live completely in the past. His spirit was a ghost, while the shell in front of me recounted war stories galore. I appreciate his service to our country, but the way he lost himself in his stories made me feel like any ear would have done. The conversation continued its slow downward spiral as he began commenting on my pregnancy. He was adamant that if he had been around, I wouldn't be pregnant. I understood his sentiment toward my circumstances, but I felt he had no right to judge. Raymond hadn't been around for my childhood. He wasn't there for me as I messed up my teenage years.

There was no way to make a comeback from the painful stabbing feeling his comments induced. I just wanted to be back home, living the nightmare I was already in, rather than this whole new one I had created for myself in Texas. I desperately wanted to run away. I wanted to ask my Aunt Beth to come get me that first night, but I chose to suck it up and stick it out at my dad's.

I stayed at my father's for three days, instead of running away like I felt he had when I was a baby. The whole time I was there, it felt like he didn't make a single feeble attempt to connect with me or even show me his town. The majority of the time I was there I watched TV, my only source of southern comfort. I had hoped he would take me to see a few sites or maybe hit up a cheap diner to try the local food. But, no. Nothing. Sadly, the visit was not the exploration of self or family history that I had hoped it would be. My dad closed himself off emotionally, so I physically shut myself in his room where I spent most of my time.

The visit dragged into Thanksgiving. I had never wished to be home more than when I found myself sadly pushing boxed mashed potatoes around my plate. I imagined my family in Pennsylvania sitting around the table as I reached for a glass of water to swallow the dry turkey in front of me. For the first time in my life, I fully appreciated the always-enjoyable homemade food we always had for the holiday. Did I really miss home? I never imagined I would feel that way.

The whole experience couldn't have been more different than what I had imagined it would be like. I had started looking for my dad years earlier. Once I had even gone on one of those people finder sites to locate him and asked my mom to pay the twenty-five dollars to obtain locked information. The information I got was about a man who earned a six-figure salary, who had no family in the surrounding area. The great power of the Internet only feeds you so much, if you don't have much information to begin with. The identity and background of the man it gave me was not my father, but I had wanted so badly to believe it was that I built the rest of my fantasy around that illusion.

Despite all the negativity, I decided it was time to forget about the bad and concentrate on the good. The one bright spot of the trip was that I learned I had another blood relative. My half sister, Mikaila Rae. Instead of wallowing in the past, I would focus on the future. I had a baby on the way and a boyfriend with whom I wanted to start building a future. Also, I now had a sister, someone untainted by the drama of our unconventional family. Maybe together we could rise above all this dysfunction and be a family.

7

Fat or Pregnant?

16 *and Pregnant* showed only a small part of my story. There are so many little details from that period of my life that I wish could have been shown. Like the fact that I was the only pregnant girl in a very small high school, which made my stomach stick out a bit—both figuratively and literally. Or that the desks at school were too small for my big belly to fit comfortably into, which felt like a big joke at my expense. Or all the ignorant babble and gossip about me. The only thing worse than being stuck in one of those desks was having to put up with all the stares and whispers.

"Is she just fat or is she pregnant?"

My classmates actually had the audacity to approach my friends with that question. Wasn't my round belly obvious enough? But the ignorance of my peers was the least of my problems. I could handle shocking or disappointing them, but there was one person I didn't want to let down. He was my favorite teacher and the only mentor I ever had.

Mr. Koser was one of the few adults I trusted. I had been in his web design class for two years and during that time we had grown close. For the first time in my life I had been able to open up to someone. He knew about my issues with my mother, but never spoke ill of her. He helped me to understand that she had her own demons shadowing her and reminded me that it was not my fault. He taught me to put my best foot forward, even if that meant letting go of the person dragging me down. He was the one person I felt wouldn't judge me, but despite that (or maybe because of it) Mr. Koser was the last person I wanted to find out that I was pregnant.

For months I avoided his hallway, hoping if he didn't see me he wouldn't find out the truth. I even begged friends who were in his class not to whisper a word about my pregnancy around him. Although part of me knew he would find out eventually—especially when all you had to do was look at me to see I was pregnant—I did everything I could to put that moment off as long as possible. Failure had never been a worry of mine because I had nobody in my life to let down. Now for the first time, I knew the heaviness of disappointing someone I looked up to. I imagined him shaking his head at me and saying something like, "You're better than this," or, "You had such a bright future. How are you going to make it now?"

By the time I had dug up enough courage to tell him, I was close to leaving school for the year. I was only a month away from giving birth so I didn't have to say much to explain my situation. Rumors had reached his ears, despite my best attempts at keeping things hushed up. To my relief, Mr. Koser didn't utter a negative word. He was one of the few people who still believed in me. I feared his disappointment more than my own mother's, but I was wrong to worry. Mr. Koser reassured me I would get through every hurdle and obstacle in my way. To this day, he's still in my life.

♦

With that behind me, I was able to move forward with my life. I had met with a school counselor and figured out a graduation plan. Since my last high school had required more credits, it turned out I had enough to finish the year early. I would graduate in January and walk with my class in May, after the baby was born. With high school now a part of the past and the extra stress of schoolwork and gossip behind me, I was able to focus on getting ready for the baby.

The crazy, hyperactive days that followed weren't enough to stop my mind from being consumed by doubt. I was still trying to convince myself that I was doing the right thing by raising a child at such a young age and sharing all of my struggles. Everyone in my life had strong opinions about what I should or shouldn't be doing. The one person who made absolutely no sense to me then, but who I later realized actually had it right the whole time, was my grandmother. She just said, "You know, babies are born!" In her weird way she was pointing out that having a child is just a part of life and now that it was a fact in mine I just had to keep moving forward.

My life wasn't going to go back to the way it was even after my baby was born. My body might go back to the way it was (well it sort of would, with hard work), but from that moment on I would be responsible for another life. Oddly, that responsibility wasn't as scary to me as it might be to others. What I was starting to realize was that this baby was going to give me a chance to have real family, to have someone who would never leave me.

Despite the chaos and uncertainty of my circumstances, I was definitely starting to feel a deep maternal connection to my baby. I still wished I was at least a decade older, but the experience of being pregnant was so intense and magical nothing could prevent me from appreciating the beauty of it. The existential experience of having a life growing inside of me turned each individual kick into shock waves that I felt throughout my whole body. There is no relationship that can compare. It's symbiotic. It's unspoken love. I was never alone anymore. When Jo left me in the middle of the night or my mom wouldn't speak to me, there was no endless emptiness. I had someone with me at all times.

The pure beauty of it all was truly a miracle to me. The world as I had known it wasn't magical or filled to the brim with good wishes and happiness. But now, for the first time in my life, I suddenly found my life filled with something I had never known before: hope. Hope that I could be a good mother. Hope for a happy future with my child.

But what would that future be? Would I be able to attend higher education? That was always my first question when I saw pregnant teens. How is she going to finish school so she can provide for her baby? I decided that I wouldn't allow myself to turn into a statistic. I would push past the odds and not let numbers decide my future.

Meanwhile, although I may have obtained a newfound positivity when it came to my future with the baby, things with Jo were not going so well. He had been working late nights

Mr. Koser is still an important person in my life. In this photo Isaac is playing around in his classroom.

at Taco Bell and had taken a shift to the shady side. He was spending less time at home and seemed to be skipping out on his classes at Northampton Community College. I began to worry that he was doing something other than going to work or school when he left the house. I suspected he might be having an affair with one of his coworkers. Every night when I went to bed, knots formed in the pit of my stomach.

Since I didn't have a car of my own, I asked a friend to take me to Taco Bell in the middle of the night to check on Jo. This wasn't the first time I had stormed into the fast food place at a ridiculous hour. In fact, I was a repeat offender. Sometimes they'd be just working or Jo's face wouldn't make an appearance at all. I wanted to catch them doing something explicit enough that I could at least have some closure and know that I wasn't losing my mind. This time, I decided to confront Jo and his coworker directly, but they sat me down and denied anything was going on between them. I had no solid proof besides Jo's sketchy behavior to go on, so I left.

But the knot in my stomach and lump in my throat would not go away. I knew it wasn't that I was letting the pregnancy hormones control me. There was definitely a problem. Jo never wanted to spend time with me anymore or he would use sleep as an excuse to avoid me. I didn't want to resort to looking through his phone, but I was at the breaking point, so I searched it. His coworker's name and number came up in texts and calls.

During such an emotionally uncertain period in our lives, I knew mistakes were going to be made, but Jo cheating on me was a whole different book I wasn't sure I was prepared to sit through and read. Unfortunately, I had no choice. I needed answers. I finally confronted him during an appointment with my OB. Obviously, the doctor's office isn't a very appropriate place to have that kind of confrontation, but Jo was never around anymore and I felt like this was my only opportunity to find out the truth.

Since his skulking around had become too obvious to deny, Jo finally admitted that he was seeing someone behind my back. He had even gone so far as to put his uniform on when he went out and bring his regular clothes in a bag so I would think he was working when he was really meeting up with her. If anyone had a right to be in a shit state, it was me. I was preparing to have a baby and the father of my child was cheating on me. Finally, I stopped fighting back the tears and let myself break down. I felt duped, cheated, and humiliated. I was completely heartbroken.

My high school graduation day, with Isaac. I graduated early but walked with my class in June.

What was there to say to make things right? Was there anything I could do to make the wrongs better? I felt trapped by Jo's lies and his feelings for this stranger. His behavior wasn't all that surprising. He was running from the serious situation we were put in and I was really frightened he would choose this other girl over me and the baby. I still loved him and I had no idea how important this other "relationship" was to him.

Once, he didn't come home until eight in the morning. It was the morning of my baby shower. I woke up, surprised to not see his usual slumped-over body staring out the window. Was he out running an errand this early after working so late? Peering outside, I saw his car enter the development. He disappeared for a minute, circling the block, and entered the driveway from the opposite direction. Jo's parents were aware that he hadn't come home the night before and when he walked in the door we all confronted him. Jo barely seemed to flinch and just shut us out, insisting that nothing had happened.

Did I want to be with someone who was capable of leaving me at such a vulnerable time? The uncertainty about our relationship that had consumed me when I first found out that I was pregnant had become relevant again. But now I worried that, even if I didn't want to be with Jo, would anyone want to be with *me* once I had a child? But at that point, it was too late to step back and rethink the biggest decision of my life. I was having this baby with or without Jo. Seconds, minutes, days flew by as my due date approached. It felt like I didn't even have a second to stop and blink.

8

THE PERSISTENT PUSH

JANUARY 18, 2010

Five a.m. was way too early to be rising; even the sun wasn't ready to begin a new day. My bladder had woken me up just as Jo was preparing to leave for work. His mom had scored him a job installing copy and fax machines in New Jersey, far away from all the drama associated with his old job. Not only did it put an end to the affair, Jo was now receiving a higher pay and benefits and his hours were earlier and more regular.

It wasn't unheard of for me to be waking up with Jo due to some pregnancy related issue. Per usual, I was exhausted and just wanted my head to be back on the pillow, but my pajamas and bed were damp so I thought I had peed myself. After cleaning up and changing, I went back to bed, but within a few hours I was woken up again by painful cramping. Pain and discomfort are pretty standard for a woman closing in on her due date, so I didn't really realize what these cramps meant.

I called my mom to ask if mild cramping was typical. She came over right away, calmly explaining to me that I was in labor and had been for hours. I was in labor? I couldn't wrap my head around it. I thought that my water breaking would be this intense moment, not just a feeling that I had wet myself. This was it? Okay. I went with the flow and followed protocol. I called my doctor. Since my contractions (the cramping I was feeling) were already five minutes apart, he told me to go to the nearest hospital, not the one I was scheduled to give birth at. We arrived at Sacred Heart Hospital at around 10:00 or 11:00 that morning and they confirmed that my water had broken. There was no denying it now, I was definitely in labor.

The boring, painful hours ticked by. I was anxious that something would go wrong, but I tried to relax and focus on the birth instead of worrying about problems over which I had no control. Soon Jo and his family arrived, accompanied by three people from the MTV crew. Even though, instead of the usual giant cameras that had been following me around, they used three handheld Flip cameras, the additional people and cameras made me feel trapped and anxious to deliver the baby.

In my episode of *16 and Pregnant* time was compressed so that the birth seemed like it happened in neat, time-segmented clips. The professionals crave certain angles and go above and beyond the regular, shaky video a family member would have shot, but what you didn't get to see were the hours of lying around in pain, hoping the delivery would speed up. In the early hours I was anxious, but not complaining yet. Every second, minute, and hour that passed was leading up to the tiny moment in time that I had been waiting so patiently for. What was one hour or two more? Besides the pain and restlessness, I was consumed by a fear that had been on my mind from the moment I had found out I was pregnant.

Throughout my pregnancy I had been worried about the baby's health. There was nothing to indicate I had any reason to be concerned, but I still had an unsettling feeling that made me question my actions left and right. Every pregnancy myth became fact in my mind and I worried constantly that my baby might not turn out to be okay. I even convinced myself that finding out the sex was bad luck. I was the only girl from my season of *16 and Pregnant* to keep the sex of the baby a surprise. I painted the nursery a neutral color and for the baby shower registry kept everything unisex. I also had a name picked out for each gender.

I don't think anyone really understood my decision, not even Jo. That age-old question,"Do you want a boy or a girl?" was tiresome to me. I didn't care. Healthy was the only thing that mattered because I had so much anxiety that I might have a baby with special medical needs. All I wanted was a strong, healthy baby. Now that I was about to give birth, I was faced with finding out if my fears had an ounce of truth to them.

After a day of labor, I had grown sick of ice chips. Although I desperately needed sustenance and water, for the most part I could deal with the pain. It wasn't excruciating until the contractions started coming nonstop. At eight centimeters dilated I was begging for an epidural to relieve the pain I had been suffering through. An epidural is an injection of anesthesia into the spine that provides pain relief for the lower half of the body. Originally, I was set on having a natural birth, but by this point the pain had become so unbearable

I realized there was no way I could get through the delivery without one.

Finally, my doctor was telling me it was time to start pushing. In front of seven people and three Flip cameras, I began the most physically demanding process of my life. *Push, Kail. Push.* The nurses, the doctor, my mom, and Jo all encouraged me. I hated those words. *Shut up! Shut up!* In the midst of the cramping and pushing an individual out of my body, I demanded absolute silence. Is that too much to ask? Finally, the voices all around me quieted down, but the cameras were still there. They seemed to hover three inches from my makeup-free face the whole time. Up until then, I hadn't had any serious regrets about having my life documented, but my mood toward that was changing. I wanted to cry.

At 6:15 p.m., Isaac Elliott was born at six pounds and four ounces. Jo cut the cord like a proper father and announced the arrival of our boy. My stomach deflated slightly. I was a mother. Now I cried.

I held Isaac, who was wrapped tightly in a hospital blanket, for an all too brief moment and glimpsed his angel face before the nurses took him away from me. His umbilical cord had been wrapped around him and as a result there was no typical shrill cry. I knew something was wrong, but I didn't really understand why he was being taken from me. I wanted to forever hold that image of his beautiful face in my head. How did I create such a perfect, little human being? The beauty cancelled out all wrongs. The endless fights and many mistakes along the way vanished miraculously the moment I saw my son. I was left to be a clutter of joy, sadness, and exhaustion.

Over the next few days I experienced such incredible sadness. I no longer had a ball of life reminding me by way of kicks and hiccups that we were one. That same little baby I had nurtured in my body was now suffering from severe jaundice, causing his skin and the whites of his eyes to yellow. The reason for the alarming color was that, because Isaac was born nearly a month early, his liver wasn't fully developed enough to break down enzymes. Wrapped up in a blue light that resembled a glowworm, he underwent phototherapy treatment in order to decrease the levels of bilirubin in his blood (build up of which in newborns can be dangerous). In those first few days, I was only allowed to see him and hold him for a few hours each day.

My anxiety was building fast as the problems with Isaac began to stack up. On top of the jaundice, the doctor was concerned that the soft spot on his head was very small. There was a possibility he had premature fusion of the skull. In other words, Isaac might end up mentally handicapped if the development of his brain was stunted by the growth of his skull. He would need to be closely examined at every check up until they could rule out the possibility.

I was scared to death. It felt like my worst fears were becoming a reality, but I tried to relax and focus on the normal aspects of becoming a new mother, like learning how to burp Isaac and change his diaper. This was the first time I ever had to change one, so it was a little bit of a challenge. Maneuvering the baby and trying to secure the diaper is especially difficult with a newborn. My first priority was to make sure my delicate son was safely lying down. As I was slowly securing the diaper, he got me. Yup, he peed all over me. My little boy was a pistol.

Three days later, I was back at Jo's house and more alone than I had been in the hospital because Jo and Janet had gone back to work. At least in the hospital there were nurses an earshot away. Now I was all on my own and, with only the help of Google to answer my endless questions, I had to learn to get by. Scared doesn't even begin to describe the nervous energy coursing through my body. How was I going to take care of this tiny baby on my own?

Changing Isaac was my biggest issue. He was so fragile, still in the fetal position. It was like pulling apart a doll made out of glass. Would I break him if I didn't spend twenty minutes gently uncurling his tiny body from the natural womb position? Hurting my baby seemed so easy to do, but I was determined to do everything necessary to prevent that from ever happening.

People had warned me motherhood was hard, but nothing could have prepared me for the mommy obstacle course of diaper genies, projectile vomit, and insistent crying. I found myself frequently using the floor of Isaac's nursery as a bed. Only getting a couple hours of sleep a night became the norm. Thankfully, maternal instincts quickly kicked in to help with my adjustment to this new lifestyle and I willingly made all those little sacrifices that are a part of normal motherhood. Tears, throw up, and poopy diapers aside, I would do it all over and over again. Sleep or no sleep, I loved this little boy. I had discovered unconditional love. The purest form of unconditional love is the love you have for your child and now I had that. I was by his side every moment, so if Isaac ever needed me, I'd be there.

Even though we lived under a roof with other people, it sometimes felt like Isaac and I were alone. We were lone rangers together. I tried to convince myself I wanted it that way—if I learned to take care of Isaac on my own I'd be ready for single motherhood if need be—but honestly I was deeply lonely. I wanted to believe that I didn't want to be bothered by visitors, but the truth is, there was no one around to help in those grueling first days. Jo and Janet returned to work immediately after Isaac's birth, so I was alone every day until about 7:00 or 8:00 in the evening. The perceived abandonment felt perversely good because I was so fueled up on stress and hormones I was dismissing the sensible side of me that normally would have recognized that social interaction is healthy. It wasn't until some of my friends came to visit that I finally peeled off my pajamas and combed my hair. I had no time in these early days for luxuries like hair straighteners or eyelash curlers.

♦

Amidst the crazy excitement and stress of those early days, *16 and Pregnant* continued filming. Through the two months after Isaac was born, the patterns of arguments and struggles began. Like many other teen mothers, I was definitely feeling isolated and trapped at home. Jo and I were fighting relentlessly over everything, from whose turn it was to get up and check on Isaac to our future together. I was frustrated because I felt like at least he was able to leave the situation for a bit by going to school and work, whereas I was stuck inside all the time.

The lack of structure, made the days long and monotonous and having no car cut me off from having a social life. The complete freedom I was used to from such a young age had been taken away and I felt like I was becoming a housewife—except that I wasn't actually Jo's wife. I had nothing of my own. I had no money, no car, no job, and no life.

I wanted to be independent and not rely on anyone, just like I always had been in the past. The enclosed environment I was living in was close to killing me. I appreciated Jo's family for taking me in, but the situation was taking a toll on our already deteriorating relationship. We were never able to resolve our problems on our own. Because we were living under their roof, his parents were involved in every spat. As soon as Jo and I raised our voices, Janet and Eddie would be there for better or for worse. They would immediately state who was right or wrong in the argument and choose a side. Janet's advice began to sound like commands to me on how to handle myself and how I should parent Isaac. The constant interference contributed to our destruction.

All I really had was Jo's family because it seemed like my mom was never around, not even to help with Isaac. This made me completely dependent on them. Although I was so grateful to Jo's parents for the support they had given me, there was a part of me that was deeply frustrated by my dependency on them.

Finally, after over four months of living with the cameras, filming of the show was done and I was hopeful things would start to calm down. Jo and I didn't resent each other, as my episode of *16 and Pregnant* made it seem through our rough patches. During the filming of the show, we fought a lot because of all the stress, but after the cameras left things settled down and our relationship improved.

A few weeks later on Valentine's Day, a friend of ours was celebrating his birthday and Jo and I actually had the opportunity to step out of the mommy and daddy zone for a bit and be social. It was difficult for both of us to go out together, so Jo offered to throw a little celebration in the basement. He seemed to be having fun, a word we weren't accustomed to anymore. The party was normal, maybe too normal. When Jo asked me to go upstairs with him, I obliged. I sensed he was up to something but I had no idea what. He slipped a small box out from his sock drawer and opened it to reveal his mother's engagement ring. Jo explained to me that Isaac's birth had changed him in ways he hadn't expected. He wanted to move on from all the negativity with me by his side as his wife. I was being asked to be part of his family officially. I was extremely shocked because Jo and I had never discussed marriage or even engagement. We had done plenty of growing up in the past few months and getting engaged seemed like a positive and happy step forward, so I said yes. Jo attempted to slip the gold-dipped ring onto my right hand as I stuck out the left one. I hoped he wasn't too embarrassed that he'd gone for the wrong hand.

With that, it started to feel like my luck was finally turning around. The stitches were healing in the wounds Jo and I had dug open over the past year. Best of all, Isaac's doctor told us we didn't need to worry about the soft spot on his head anymore. But, just as the worries I had about Isaac's health were beginning to fade, something horrible happened. At four months old, Isaac had a seizure in my lap.

There was no warning. All the most awful stories start out on a normal day during an everyday activity. Unfortunately, that's how Isaac's first seizure happened. Isaac was on my lap and I was trying to play with him and bond as usual. He'd laugh here and there but I couldn't get much out of him, which was a tad on the unusual side. Was he getting sick? Suddenly, Isaac's movements came to a halt. He went limp and his eyes rolled back. Then he threw up. I immediately dialed 911.

People showed up, even my mom and her boyfriend, but I don't remember calling anyone. I don't even remember if Jo and Janet were home at that point. It's all a blur. All I know is that as the ambulance rolled up to the house, nothing mattered but Isaac. My little baby was very sick and for a mother there is no bigger fear. Riding in the back of the ambulance with him made my stomach turn into a jumble, and the bumpy road we were driving on had nothing to do with it. Was this my fault? Did I do something wrong? It was easier to blame myself than to think that it could just be the randomness of the universe.

In the end, the doctors couldn't answer my questions or pinpoint the cause of Isaac's seizures. We stayed in the hospital for four days and then followed up with a neurologist a couple times, but the scans revealed nothing. The lack of sleep made me emotional and I would lash out wildly, usually at Jo. I wanted to cry every time I looked at Isaac. The haunting image of him hooked up to machines with countless wires coming out of his tiny body was enough for any mother to lose it. He was only four months old and going through more than some adults ever have to endure.

During the four days we spent in the hospital, Isaac had an EKG, EEG, MRI, and CAT scan. But none of those tests gave me any solace or even much information to go on. Isaac had one more seizure during his stay at the hospital. The doctors were there to witness it this time, yet there was nothing they could tell me. The seizures weren't febrile, which ruled out fevers being the trigger. The doctors also confirmed that Isaac did not have epilepsy, a serious neurological disorder. Thankfully Isaac hasn't had a seizure since we left the hospital. My concern levels never dropped, though. I will always worry, even when Isaac goes off to college.

♦

All things considered, I had to start thinking about my future. I was a getting tired of being a puppet and not walking on

Me and Isaac.

my own without strings. Since I had no car, I felt like I had to ask permission to take Isaac out. I couldn't pay for anything, which made me feel like I couldn't validate my opinions. I didn't say much. I didn't eat too much. I didn't go out without asking. Dependency is not always healthy. Why do you think they named those adult diapers after the word?

By this point, the illusion of being in love with Jo was wearing off. I used to truly believe we had a chance. The more I matured, the more I changed. I wanted freedom from the monotonous days and ultimately from Jo. I wanted to be a good mother to Isaac and live under no one else's authority. I couldn't do that with Jo, especially living under his parents' roof.

Meanwhile, *16 and Pregnant* had aired and using the episode to reflect back was unhealthy in some ways. I didn't want to dwell on the past when I needed to live in the present tense. Watching the footage of Isaac's birth was both beautiful and heart wrenching. It was a reminder of how ill he was, but also how far we had come. Watching his name, *Isaac Elliot*, appear across the screen brought back the joy I felt in the moment he was born. I smirked as the normal gestational weeks were posted as if I had gone through a perfectly standard labor. I never went full term. I guess somewhere in the editing they got it mixed up.

Nonetheless, the beauty of childbirth gave me chills. I was so lucky to have professionals film my experience. Although it pales in comparison, we do have a shaky, homemade version just in case Isaac ever wants to see a different point of view. For the most part, looking back at the footage was helpful. I realized the positive certainly outweighed the negative experiences from pregnancy up until birth.

Watching my life on television, the fights with Jo and the hardships we endured, was painful but it definitely helped me gain some perspective. I felt like I had grown since then, but not enough. I wanted to have a place of my own and a car so I could drive to work and support my son. The steps I was taking toward a better future weren't advancing my life as quickly as I had hoped. Jo and me constantly teetering back and forth wasn't helping either. By this point, we were finished falling back into each other's arms. We ended the engagement after only three or four months.

I focused on job hunting and found a position at Sports Authority. A few weeks later I received another phone call from MTV. They were offering me a chance to be part of the *16 and Pregnant* spinoff series, *Teen Mom.* I wasn't sure if Jo would be on board to be under a microscope once again, this time over a much longer period of time, but for me, there wasn't much to contemplate. My living situation at the time wasn't making me happy and, since nothing too negative had come out of filming *16 and Pregnant*, it seemed like *Teen Mom 2* would be a huge opportunity for me to do something positive with my life.

9

SINGLE TO HOMELESS

The boat was rocking. Tipping to the left and then to the right. I eased into each direction in order not to lose my balance completely. There was no ocean, only a sea of people. Jo and his family were on one side, while a new arrival in my life was on the other. I would have to choose and that choice would have a major impact on both my life and Isaac's.

Leaving Jo had crossed my mind often but I just never had the courage to go through with it. I got a job at Sports Authority and because of the confidence I got from working there I was beginning to feel like I could stand on my own two feet. This newfound sense of independence helped me to see that I didn't have to settle for how I was living.

Jo's family accepting me was the closest I had ever come to being a part of a loving family, but I was beginning to realize

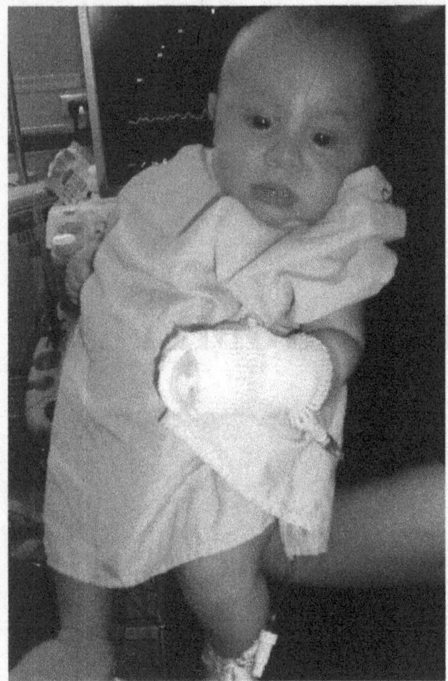

Isaac during his stay in the hospital for seizures.

that I had made myself believe I needed his family because I didn't have a supportive family of my own. I had grown so tired of constantly trying to fit into Jo's family, but more than that, I was done lying. I had become friends with a guy named Jordan, one of my coworkers at Sports Authority. Hanging out with Jordan was refreshing and fun, even if at first he seemed like he wasn't exactly the smartest of the pack. He was a great person and our friendship was a hundred percent healthier than anything I ever had with Jo. But spending time with Jordan, friends or not, was difficult because I felt like I had to lie. Even though I was working, the reality of a minimum wage job was that I couldn't contribute much to

Swimming with Isaac.

the household. I was still very much dependent on Jo's parents at this point and I knew they wouldn't approve of me hanging out with some guy they'd never met.

Even a day at the beach meant weaseling around so Jo and his family wouldn't find out. I felt guilty for wanting to get away for a while, but it had nothing to do with Jordan. The fact of the matter was I needed some time for myself. This period of sneaking around didn't even last as long as a typical celebrity marriage. Jo quickly noticed my attraction and attention sway, so he began focusing on me again. He wanted me to chase him to resume the game of back and forth girlfriend. Jo spent more time talking to me and pushed the conversation into the direction of working our kinks out as a couple. But by then I had already moved on. Isaac deserved to have a happy family, not two miserable young adults hiding behind polite smiles.

♦

At first, I didn't want to be completely honest with Jo in case Jordan and I decided not to become serious. It was a very big deal to me, too. This would be the first relationship I had been in since Isaac was born. That being said, I knew not talking about it would only make the conversation much harder in the future. Uncomfortably, we discussed the nature of my relationship with Jordan. It didn't seem like much of a secret I was spilling. After breaking up with Jo, it was only a matter of time before one of us moved on. Jo's parents weren't thrilled about me dating, but this also meant Jo would be dating soon, too. It was the golden break we needed in our complicated lives.

Once I cleared the air with Jo and his parents, Jordan and I were free to date. We chose not to rush into a relationship so our friendship could blossom first. I decided we should wait to have sex and even after three months we were going strong without it. It was comforting to have found someone who was willing to wait until I was ready. Although, eventually, he did become impatient. Like most guys, he succumbed to the belief that having a girlfriend was pointless if sex wasn't part of the relationship. The waiting had proved to me that sex didn't have to be the epicenter of our relationship, but I understood to a degree that it was important to him and gave in.

It turned out I was right to take a chance on Jordan. He was a person I could truly count on. I found myself liking him more each day as he kept me on my toes and always found the fun in everything. This relationship was unlike anything I had ever experienced. We kept busy. We actually had adventures as a couple instead of holing up all the time. We went out to eat, saw movies, shopped, and took trips to the beach. Later, as his involvement increased with MTV, we traveled to New York and Los Angeles together.

My decision to leave Jo meant I had to move out of his parent's house. I had been living in their basement ever since we had broken up, but the change of rooms was a temporary solution to a growing problem. Eventually, I just ditched my belongings in the spare room in their basement and house hopped. No matter what the circumstances were I didn't want to take advantage of the hospitality and generosity his family had shown me. I opted to stay at my mom's whenever possible and at Jordan's on the other days. Obviously, I couldn't go on like that indefinitely. I needed my own place, but supporting myself and Isaac on a single, minimum wage income wasn't realistic.

Thankfully, there are resources out there for young mothers like me. Valley Youth House, an organization that provides intervention services and counseling for young people, has a housing program for single mothers but they required a two-day stay in a homeless shelter in order to qualify. I was very wary about staying in a shelter even temporarily, but Isaac was my main concern. He needed a safe place to live with me and, at that point, staying at a homeless shelter for two nights seemed like a small price to pay. I already met their requirement of working at least twenty hours a week and not having a safe, permanent residence. This was one of the last prerequisites I needed to check off to qualify for the program.

I arranged for Isaac to stay at Jo's, but I kept everyone in the dark as to where I was going. The shelter was in an old Victorian home in a not so great part of town. Since I still didn't have a car, I asked Jordan to drive me there. I lied to him, saying I was doing a project—some good old-fashioned community service—but the backpack I brought didn't have a notebook or log in sheet. Just a blanket, pillows, a few overnight supplies, and a phone charger. These were my temporary home fixtures.

The room I was given was large and impersonal. The mattress was stiff and thin. I wasn't expecting a Posturepedic or heated blanket, but it was still hard to be in a place like that. I felt so restless and uncomfortable. Maybe these feelings were coming from within, from feeling ashamed of where I was. Nobody knew what I was doing, not even the MTV producers, and I hoped it would remain that way because I felt like utter shit.

The next day I went to work. I wouldn't answer Jordan's question as to why I needed to be dropped off again in Easton. I put on a happy face, but being in a homeless shelter was depressing. I couldn't imagine spending more than the weekend there, yet most of the people there wanted and needed more than just a few days. The shelter had a thirty-day maximum stay, but everyone around me seemed to be begging for an extension. I wanted to believe the best but I overheard conversations about scheming the system. My heart went out to the innocent children who had done no wrong. They deserved better. I avoided looking into their eyes and shut myself into my room for the night.

There was an 11:00 p.m. curfew and no TV, so I changed my sleeping patterns and shut my eyes early. If I had to pee, I held it in. I refused to use the bathroom or the shower. This had nothing to do with pride. I really had no idea if these closed-off rooms were ever cleaned or if any dirty scenarios played out in there. I just wanted to shut my eyes and forget that I had ever been there.

I was able to get through it because I was motivated by a need for independence. I was determined never to have to rely on anyone ever again. I had to be strong for Isaac.

I would never allow my son to become one of those children in the shelter, hoping in vein for a brighter future. The amount I learned in the two days I stayed in the shelter was worth more than all the money in the world. It's so easy to get caught up in your own life and tribulations, but there is always somebody out there who has it worse than you do. The payoff in my day-to-day life was tangible, too. The housing program would help me pay rent as long as I maintained a full-time job. Since I was already working, I was set. I found a reasonable apartment to live in and signed a one-year lease. The freedom of having my own place was like flying.

Just like that, the solitude to which I had grown so accustomed disappeared. Jordan began spending the majority of his time with me and was pretty much unofficially living with me in my new apartment. Finding a huge white tee or a pair of boxers mixed in with the laundry wasn't so unusual anymore. Jordan was a huge help. He quickly bonded with Isaac and even Jo grew to like him.

10

REGRETS

As my relationship with Jordan turned into a strong partnership, we found we had a new challenge to deal with. We had caught the attention of the paparazzi and, on Isaac's first birthday, I had one of the inhuman stalkers follow me from Jo's house to my apartment. I freaked out. They knew my address. They knew where my baby lived. Why were they following me? I'm not a celebrity. *Teen Mom 2* filming aside, I felt like my baby was totally off limits. But the paparazzi seemed to have missed the memo.

After that my guard was up, even while doing the simplest things like leaving work, doing laundry, or grocery shopping. I resented this invasion of my privacy. Although I had signed a contract with MTV to share certain aspects of my life, I hadn't signed up for the public to have twenty-four-hour access to my life. But the popularity of *Teen Mom*

2 meant that details about our personal lives had become a valuable commodity. People wanted to know more about us, and the tabloids would go to any lengths to get their customers what they wanted. I was okay with that as long there were some boundaries. I didn't want my entire life publicized. Unfortunately, I was quickly learning that I didn't really have a choice.

I felt bad for Jordan because he truly had no idea what he had signed up for when we started dating. But, despite how being in the public eye was impacting his life, he made it clear to me that he intended to be there next to me for the whole journey. Jordan was my sidekick and a rock for me as the ratings for *Teen Mom 2* soared and I became the subject of media scrutiny. Meanwhile, because Jordan was now a regular on the show, he was developing a fan base of his own. We received countless well wishes to our future on Twitter, which were more than welcome. However, some girls took it to a level I wasn't comfortable with and Jordan was a little too friendly for my liking. One girl in particular was acting like she was making plans to move in with Jordan. I felt really hurt and almost angry at Jordan. This girl wanted to live with him just because she saw him on television. He had so many amazing qualities and she wanted him for something so stupid.

After such a solid year together, I was disappointed that Jordan had become so caught up in the attention that the show had brought him. I don't think he had any real intention of going through with this move, but at the time I couldn't help but leap to conclusions. I really loved him so the betrayal stung. But, I couldn't really confront him about it without being a hypocrite. The small mistakes Jordan made weren't seen on television, but my huge downfall was.

Doing laundry with Isaac.

My heart may have belonged to Jordan, but there were pieces I never took back from Jo. Because of Isaac we had a deep connection and an intense shared history. For the first time since I found out I was pregnant, we were getting along smoothly. Because we had never learned how to be friends, we fell back into old habits and I cheated on Jordan with Jo. Even though I was deeply in love with Jordan, I selfishly wanted Jo to remain single. I had typical girl syndrome: I didn't want Jo, but I also didn't want anyone else to be with him. One night, after he dropped Isaac off, we slept together. Jordan arrived home from work earlier than expected and he knew almost immediately what happened.

Cheating never leads to a happy ending. It certainly didn't for us. Cheating on someone is a heavy burden, worse than any other mistake you can make in a relationship. Cheating is cold, selfish, and heartless. I had committed a cardinal sin in my book. You'd be surprised sometimes what you're capable of. Jo and I were finished. We weren't getting back together and the hook up didn't signify a change in that. I wanted to work it out with Jordan so we tried to recover from the betrayal. There was the predictable breakup, and the even more predictable getting back together. I still deeply regret that I put Jordan in that position. He didn't deserve to have an arrow shot through his heart only to have it ripped out again.

But, at the same time, Jordan was changing. When we first started dating, Jordan rarely drank, but now he was partying all the time. Since he was young and carefree, he had a right to do that, but I didn't have that luxury, so I decided that we needed to break up permanently. In the year and a half that we were a couple, I took away a life's worth of lessons about how to function in a healthy relationship. It was easily the most stable relationship I had ever been in and knowing I was capable of having that in my life was a blessing. I was sad I had to say goodbye to someone I considered to be such a great, dependable person. Now, there was nobody in my life I could depend on.

♦

After Jordan and I broke up, I met I guy who had a detrimental effect on me. We were not dating, just casually seeing each other once in a while. We weren't sexually active, so minds out of the gutter. Caleb had been asking me out on a date and I had finally said yes. After I had blown him off multiple times, I figured one date wouldn't be the worst thing ever. Just like most guys want sex, most girls want to be loved and I was no exception.

One night, Caleb came over to my apartment. He was plastered and insisted he needed to talk to me so I let him in. But he had no interest in talking. He pulled me into the bedroom and slammed me onto the bed, taking my clothes off roughly. I screamed and tried to shove him off, ordering him to stop touching me, but I was no match for his tall, muscular frame. His strength was so overpowering, I could barely move. I felt a tear and knew I was bleeding. When he finished, he left me in tears, screaming for him to leave.

I was in a state of shock. It felt like I was dead. The blood-stained sheets snapped me back to reality and I realized I wasn't okay, even if I was still alive. I didn't know what to do, so I called the only person I could trust. Jordan rushed me to the hospital. He wanted to know what had happened, but I couldn't talk about it—not even to the doctors. I was so torn up inside, I needed stitches sewn with the thickest thread they could find. The pain was excruciating. My nerves were shot. Although the doctors knew what had happened to me, I wouldn't give them permission to use the rape kit. I was set free—contrary to how I felt—to go home.

As Jordan drove me home, I was still in a state of shock. I wasn't able to fully process what had just happened to me. Doing the right thing and reporting Caleb to the police never seemed like a viable option at the hospital. Fear had taken over. What would happen to me or to Caleb if I turned him in? Would he come after me for revenge? I was afraid of all the consequences. What's even crueler was how I viewed myself. I was so disgusted, like it was *my* fault. I was a victim and classically accusing myself of having done something wrong. My usual strength and confidence vanished as fear took hold.

As days passed, the fear of seeing Caleb subsided and he never contacted me again. The damage he had done was obvious enough even to him, so he knew to stay far away. The trauma of having been raped ate away at me. Not speaking out or acknowledging how I had been violated meant that I was imprisoned by the weight of such a horrible secret. But keeping secrets with a smile was the way I had always lived. I didn't know how to break out of the pattern. *Speak up. Have a voice.* I wanted to. I wanted to shout for every single woman who has ever been touched against her will. I'm the exact example of what not to do. Admitting that has been difficult for me.

In order not to reveal the darkness I was swimming in, there was a certain of level of dishonesty I had to achieve.

Victims become numb to the world. I was lying to myself in so many different ways because I didn't want to feel. Denial is a powerful thing. There was a kind of relief to pretending I lived in a world where I wasn't a rape victim. In different shoes, I was free from the trauma of brutality. But if I allowed my mind to waver from the lie for even a second, it would all come crashing down on me. The experience caused me to withdraw, so that I could hide from this colossal secret.

Until now I have only told a handful of people about what happened. While I wasn't brave enough to turn my rapist in at the time, I want to speak out now. I am a victim. Every victim deserves to be heard. If I could rewind time I would tell myself this. I hope that by sharing my story now, I might help someone who has been a victim of rape to find a voice to speak out. Please, no matter how frightened you are, no matter what your mind tells you, just do it. Don't let anyone get away with the crime because you are worth so much more than that.

11

FIXING MY FORTUNE

On January 11, 2011 the first episode of *Teen Mom 2* aired on MTV to an audience of 3.6 million viewers. The success of the show seemed to escalate overnight. No one predicted its potential to surpass ratings of similar reality show premiers, like the original *Teen Mom.* The bigger the show grew, the more Facebook friend requests I received. I was averaging at least a hundred per week.

But even as our fans and supporters multiplied, the critics were becoming harsher. The worst for me were the hateful comments on Twitter. There were tons of hateful posts judging me on my appearance and these trolls managed to find endlessly creative and hurtful ways to call me ugly. I even had a Twitter page dedicated to me titled, "Hulk Kail." Some of the hate was generated from my actions on the show, like how I cheated on Jordan, but the rest of it was directed at my physical flaws. All that negativity and hate can be a heavy burden to carry, but I tried to rise above it rather than to allow it to drag me down.

Nevertheless, the media's capacity to dig up every dirty little secret terrified me. Mostly, I was terrified they would get hold of the story of my abortion, which at that point I was not ready to share. I had no illusions about the lengths the tabloids would go to obtain a story—they had already begun contacting anyone who had a few degrees of separation from me.

Despite all that negativity, and on top of everything I was already struggling with, I managed to keep my head held high—even if it was a bit wobbly. The breaking point for me came after someone posted my cell phone number on a porn website, accompanied by a naked, photoshopped picture of Jenelle, one of the other girls featured on *Teen Mom 2*. I believe they wanted to pass the photo off as me, but despite how ridiculous this was, my phone started blowing up with calls from California to China. At first I answered the calls, not knowing who could possibly be on the other end of the phone. I regretted it immediately. The string of calls were from sleazy guys saying explicitly sexual things about the photo. The person who put my information out on the Internet clearly intended for me to become the target of harassment. The bullying was terrible. Being harassed from around the world was definitely a new experience, but one I'd sooner not have had. In addition to the porn site, my number was posted on Craigslist as though I were selling a mini fridge. The disturbing thing was that the person behind the posting must have been someone close to me. Otherwise, how would they have gotten hold of my private cell number?

No matter how hard I tried to rise above it all, incidents like this began to eat away at me. I took every comment to heart and even considered deleting my Twitter account. Not only was I listening to people who really knew nothing about me, I actually began to believe their negative opinions. Like most teenage girls, I already struggled with insecurities about my self-image. Having my imperfections broadcast on television, like the days I had a skin flare up or a bloated stomach from my period, only intensified those insecurities.

Now that I was on television, I no longer had control of my own image. I hated seeing my face and my body on the TV screen. Every flaw, down to the last stray hair, was magnified by each close up shot. Most people on television have makeup artists, hair stylists, and a wardrobe team to transform them into glamorous superstars. I had a tube of mascara, a brush, and a closet full of leggings and sweatshirts. Not to say I needed any of that big production stuff, but there is a certain elegance required for the on air look and I definitely did not have the resources to pull it off.

But it wasn't just the physical that was being judged; my personality was under the microscope as well. In reality television, there is no middle ground. If you're too monotone, people accuse you of being a miserable bitch. If you're too bubbly and happy, you're accused of being a fake bitch. Without really knowing me at all, people accused me of being selfish, of being a bad mother because I warmed Isaac's milk up in the microwave. I was branded incapable of monogamy because I had cheated on Jordan with Jo. Worst of all, was how people judged my relationship with my parents. I was accused of being shallow because of my decision to cut them out of my life.

When I signed on to do *Teen Mom 2*, I had no idea how much of an affect the negative attention would have on my self-esteem. I wasn't sure anymore if I could justify the short-term pain for the long-term goal of sharing my story and helping young girls like me. I had always been my toughest critic, but I was feeling more critical of myself than ever. I let the hate soak in and allowed the negative comments to overshadow the love and support I did receive. There were times I even felt suicidal, but I managed to stabilize myself when I hit that low point.

I just needed a reminder of what the bigger picture was. It's easy to lose sight of the important things when you are so focused on the negativity of your situation. I had Isaac, my sweet, innocent boy. I was being selfish. The important lesson I have learned from that difficult period of my life is that 'tough times don't last, but tough people do.'

♦

Flying across the country was a luxury in itself. Los Angeles was a world away from what I was used to. Then again, everything that was happening in those days was completely new to me. Filming for the reunion special was more extravagant than I had expected. After I arrived in LA, I was driven to a large warehouse that had been transformed into a makeshift studio, almost like a film set. The hustle and bustle around me was mesmerizing. I couldn't believe I was part of this! Before I could really take in the atmosphere, I was shown to my own private dressing room. I definitely was not used to that kind of star treatment.

Turn on the bright lights and paint my face with makeup. It's studio television, ladies and gentlemen. I wasn't sure if adrenaline was kicking my body into high gear or if it was just the anxiety I had been struggling with over the years, but my heart was racing, beating faster with every second that we came closer to rolling. I wasn't sure if I'd be able to keep my body still enough so I didn't appear fidgety. This wasn't my first televised interview, but I doubt being in the spotlight will never feel normal.

It's pretty typical for reality television shows to have a reunion episode in which the entire cast is brought together to talk about the season and provide updates for what's happened in their lives. I had already done a similar reunion for *16 and Pregnant*, but since I had been a last minute addition to that show, meeting the other teen mothers had felt brief and disconnected.

Teen Mom 2 had narrowed the cast from that season of *16 and Pregnant* from eight down to four—Jenelle, Leah, Chelsea, and me. Now, instead of being one of many, I was a part of a much smaller cast—although, obviously we didn't film together because the show follows each of us individually in our hometowns. Although it was exciting to be part of this reunion episode, what I cared most about was getting to meet the other girls from the show. The other three girls knew one another from the *16 and Pregnant* reunion, Leah and Chelsea in particular had already passed the acquaintance stage and were able to chat comfortably. At the time, I didn't really know much about them beyond what I had seen on the show, but I hoped the *Teen Mom 2* reunion would help me to better understand the girls I had been watching on TV.

I was excited to get past the awkward beginning stages of friendship because we had all been through such similar experiences. Since none of my friends had ever been through it themselves, they couldn't relate to my life as a teen mother. On top of that, I was having my life televised, which was completely abnormal to everyone around me. Jenelle,

Chelsea, and Leah understood both. Friendship was a given in my mind. I thought it was going to be easy to connect and become instant friends and when that didn't happen I worried that we might never be friends.

At first, I had felt out of place because at the *16 and Pregnant* reunion it had felt like none of the other cast members were making an effort to talk to me and I had instinctively shut down. This time, I was determined to let down my guard. Initially, I gravitated toward the other girl who seemed to float on the same plane as me. The unpredictable Jenelle had a fighting spirit I could relate to. We became friends, while Chelsea and Leah had bonded before I even stepped into the room.

My fear of not ever connecting with the girls died faster than a flickering flame on a windy day. As Twitter had become the latest social media sensation, it really brought us together as a cast. We were able to contact each other frequently and bond over the similar positive and negative responses we were receiving through Twitter. We also exchanged numbers and talked frequently outside of the public eye. Like cliques in school, we found ourselves in one another. Chelsea turned out to be the lone ranger, who kept to herself and had to be coaxed out from her own world. She had such a shaky relationship with her child's father and I really felt for her because I had been there, too. Jenelle, as most probably knew, was the wild child who pretty much made me look like a recluse. I'm convinced no one loves Ke$ha as much as Jenelle. She's hardcore. The Southern belle, Leah, is the one I'm closest to. We actually visit each other outside of *Teen Mom 2* publicity. I was so happy when she married Jeremy because individually they are amazing but together they glow. She invited me to her wedding and it was one of the most beautiful and meaningful ceremonies I've ever attended.

Chelsea, Jenelle, and Leah became more than just my cast mates—they became my friends. We all agree that through *Teen Mom 2* there is a bigger message we hope to project. We want to make people aware of the struggles of being a teen mother, even though sometimes that message is overshadowed by the drama of our relationships. We want to be known for more than just our mistakes, but we have learned we need to be careful because we are often portrayed in the media as figures to be mocked. It may seem to people like we benefit from all the rumors and gossip about us, but the truth is, gracing the covers of tabloid magazines doesn't make our bank accounts surge, nor does it create the positive message we hope to pass on.

In an effort to turn the publicity surrounding us in a positive direction, we agreed to do interviews where we could discuss issues that were meaningful to us. We were invited to appear on *Good Morning America*, Anderson Cooper's daytime talk show, *Anderson Live*, and Dr. Drew's *Lifechangers*. To be invited onto these television shows was beyond my wildest dreams, a once in a lifetime opportunity. I loved doing it, but we did not profit financially from these appearances. Our travel expenses were covered, but that's it.

I truly enjoyed these experiences and found a new love for the camera, although I'd rather be the one asking the questions than have all that overwhelming attention on me. For the first time, I understood that there is a potential career behind what I was already doing for *Teen Mom 2*. Maybe one day I'll try working in radio or behind the scenes in television. Realistically, though, I still have to tackle the overwhelming first step—getting a college degree.

12

SISTER, SISTER

Enrolling in community college seemed like the best option for me, as I still wasn't sure what career path I wanted to pursue. I decided to seek out some counseling assistance from the school, but their recommendations were not realistic options for me. Their advice was to not have a job and to concentrate solely on my schoolwork. I would have loved to follow this advice, but in reality I was struggling to balance attending classes and keeping up with schoolwork with press outings, a child, two jobs, and filming for *Teen Mom 2*.

I changed my major quite a few times. First I tried business, but it involved way too much math so I literally walked out of my first class as the rest of the poor saps crunched numbers. Business was too practical for me. I needed passion. I was interested in social work because I wanted to help people who were struggling. Social work is a career in which the ultimate goal isn't a six-figure income. It's about helping people in need. It's loving what you do every single day. I worked at it for four semesters, but in the end I dropped out before receiving my associate degree. Reality crashed hard every morning as I struggled to get myself and Isaac out the door. I quickly became discouraged by how challenging every day truly was. I needed to be working full time as quickly as possible to support myself and my son and sadly social work meant more schooling than I could handle at that time.

So I left community college, trading in my textbooks for toothbrushes and dental floss. Becoming a dental assistant had always been in the back of my mind as a way to provide for Isaac and myself. Little did I know then that trade school would be as difficult and time consuming as community college. In order to become certified, there are weekly tests that need to be passed and a state x-ray test. I was finding it increasingly difficult to balance school with the rest of my hectic life.

During the day I was either working at a local Italian restaurant or at Sports Authority. After putting in a long shift, I'd hop on over to the Lehigh Valley School of Dental Assisting to drain whatever brain cells I had left. While I was at school or work, Isaac would be in daycare, with Jordan, or occasionally with my mom. Unfortunately, I didn't feel like I could rely on my mother and I would often come home to a cloud of cigarette smoke, wondering if the stains on the carpet were Captain Morgan. It seemed like she couldn't handle her only duty of putting Isaac to bed. I was so worried about what was going on at home that I couldn't concentrate and I would often end up calling in sick at work or skipping class so I wouldn't have to leave Isaac. Plus, I felt guilty putting so much pressure on Jordan. I was lucky to be able to call on him to be a stable figure for Isaac and it was clear he loved my little boy, but I was the mother and he was my responsibility.

Fortunately, the little support I had was enough to get by for now. Also, I felt a little more at peace now that I had stability at school and was no longer bouncing back and forth between majors. It had been such an intensely stressful situation not knowing what to choose. Because I had never been active in sports or clubs as a child, I was still figuring out who I was and what I liked as a young adult.

♦

It felt like I was still seeking the pieces of me that were missing. And I believed that a large chunk lay in Texas. I needed to know where I came from and the trip I had taken to meet my dad while I was pregnant with Isaac hadn't given me all the information I had wanted. Meeting my father didn't deter me from seeking out the rest of his family and completing my family tree. Through social media, I was able to connect with my next closest relative—my half sister, Mikaila. Despite how much information there is online, reaching out to her proved more difficult than I had expected. Eventually, though, through a line of strangers, I was able to contact her.

Originally, I was only able to obtain her brother's name. Spencer didn't have any online profiles so I felt the search was completely fruitless until one day he called me out of the blue. Initially, he had acted as a barrier to Mikaila because he was wary of what I wanted from her. He seemed worried that Raymond had sent me to open up the possibility for him to enter Mikaila's life. Once I explained I had no ties to Raymond,

Spencer let his guard down and promised to pass my contact information along. It took a while, but eventually Mikaila texted me. Immense relief and excitement welled up in my body as she expressed the same feelings of wanting to connect. However, I sensed some apprehension from her. Mikaila was four years younger than me and her mother's hesitation had made her wary of opening up to me. I understood and hoped to erase any doubts.

Texas was calling once again. The land of barbecues and George Bush just kept sucking me back in like a black hole. I hoped not to drown this time around. Bringing my family together was all I ever wanted. The disappointment I had to swallow during my original visit was still settling in my stomach. I brought Isaac along just as I had when I met my father. Only this time he was now a living, breathing baby in the outside world. Inside the bustling airport, I searched for Mikaila and her mother, trying not to think back to my last visit. This trip had to be better. It just had to.

Tears sprung from my eyes as I made eye contact with my sister for the first time. This extremely emotional moment didn't seem to faze Mikaila. Thankfully, her mother's hug consoled any quick, judgmental and negative energy on my part. After being disenchanted by my father, I hoped for a stronger bond with my half sister. Both of us had lived without a father, so I knew we had already had at least that much in common.

Outside the airport, I was feeling more positive as the hot sun beamed on my face. Maybe I was trying too hard to connect with Mikaila, but the attempts seemed so fruitless. We were two very different people and she was still so young. Her words were awkward and our differences made it difficult to communicate. The simplest things became complicated because of our major disconnection. She was a sweet girl. Why didn't we get each other? I wish it had gone differently.

Despite my worsening mood, I was relieved to be reunited with my cousins. Kaylie, Carli, and Marlin were family. Although they were older than me (all in their mid-to-late twenties) we were in similar places in our lives and it was easy to connect with them. I had met them once long ago, but I was too young to have any memory of it. I never knew what family meant until I spent time with these women. Kaylie and I bonded the most, and not just because of the crazy coincidence of our similar names. She became a sister to me and I stayed with her for the majority of the time I was in Texas.

Having my family together, like we should have been from the start, felt so right. There was no looking back, only forward. Instead of wallowing in the pain of the past, we made the most of the week. The nights we spent hanging out together in Kaylie's apartment made up for all of the childhood sleepovers we never had. I cherish those moments because of the effortless connection. I couldn't wait to come back.

As I flew home to Pennsylvania, I realized that not only did I want to go back to Texas to visit, I wanted to move there permanently some day. For the first time in my life I felt like I had a family, a place where I felt I truly belonged. In Texas, I could have reliable support for Isaac. In Pennsylvania, the family I so desperately wanted and needed would be thousands of miles away.

My cousin Kaylie Terry, me, my cousin Carli Sander, and my half sister Mikaila Shelburne.

13

LOVE COMES TO TOWN

Meanwhile, I had fallen into a rut since Jordan and I had broken up. I focused on finishing up my training to become a dental assistant, but I felt like I needed a major change in my life. We had been an on-again-and-off-again couple for a few months, but now we were for sure done. I had made that clear by changing jobs and distancing myself from him even as friends. Jordan's support as a friend showed me that he cared about Isaac and me, but as much as I appreciated his presence and help, I knew it was time to move on. I quit working at Sports Authority and found a job at a clothing store at the mall in order to concentrate on making more money.

Working at a clothing store was a challenge because of the competitive pressure of working on commission. I pounced on customers as casually as I could to make a sale and up my check. I even managed to convince one guy to purchase a shirt that cost nearly a hundred dollars! Actually, he looked about fifteen so I assumed his dad was paying for it. He ended up bringing it back the next day and sadly my check dropped a notch. From a conversation we'd had the day before, he remembered I was having my wisdom teeth removed so he asked me if he could take me out for ice cream after. It was a sweet gesture, but there was no way I was going on a date with a high school sophomore.

But Javi was persistent. He reached out to me on Twitter, and I learned that he wasn't fifteen, as I had thought, but nineteen. And his "dad" was actually his older brother, Sal. Javi was charming and forward enough to ask for my address so he could bring me ice cream on the day I had my wisdom teeth out—even though my cheeks were so swollen from the surgery, that I wasn't sure if I wanted to be seen by anyone.

At that point I still wasn't completely over the breakup with Jordan and I didn't want to admit to the excruciatingly painful feelings of liking someone new. There's no healthy way to come to terms with the start of feelings for a new person when you aren't over an old relationship. I felt like I should be focused on my career and taking care of Isaac, not getting tangled up with a new guy. But I couldn't get Javi out of my head.

After two months or so of hanging out as friends, Javi drove himself all the way to New York, where I was filming the Season 3 reunion show. At that point, I couldn't deny his attraction to me any longer. No guy would drive over two hours in Manhattan traffic for just any old girl. He was definitely falling for me. I knew I had to tell Javi very bluntly that, no matter how flattered I was, nothing was going to happen between us. While my cast mates went out on an adventure in the city, I stayed back in my hotel room to take care of a friend who'd had too much to drink. At some point Javi and I found ourselves alone in the room and we were forced into the moment I had wanted to avoid. He asked me straight up if we would ever move past friendship.

"Javi, I'm sorry. I have no intention of being with you. I just can't." But even as a said those words, inside I was conflicted. There were so many reasons, why I had to reject him. I had too much shit going on in my life. I didn't want to dump anything on Javi. He deserved to have a normal start to a relationship. But, despite all that, there was a part of me that couldn't help being drawn to this guy who was unlike anyone I had ever met.

"I respect that, but I will always be here as a friend for you." Javi was perfect. He had driven over two hours to get this lousy response from me; yet his reaction was so sweet and virtuous. Great. Javi was one of the good guys. That just made everything so much worse.

I pretended to smile and saved the tears for my hotel bedroom's pillow. I wasn't over Jordan yet, and Javi deserved more than a rebound relationship. Back home, I distanced myself from Javi, but the feelings I had for him refused to go away. My past experiences with guys had been so complicated and painful, that I had reached the point where I actually hated myself for falling in love with someone. The way I was falling for Javi was different from the way I had felt about Jo or Jordan. There was a natural transition from friendship to something deeper. The more he showed me about himself, the more I liked him.

If I wanted to move forward I had to answer one question. Would I ever be able to be sexually involved again? Having sex with someone would make me physically and emotionally vulnerable and I wasn't sure I was in the right state to be either. The rape had become a giant steel wall that kept me from feeling anything for anyone. What I didn't realize then was that this wall wasn't truly protecting me, it was just another impediment to my future happiness.

That winter, despite my determination to stay away, Javi and I became friends. The more time I spent with him, the more I gradually began to feel again. Living up to his words to me that night in New York, he had been a true friend those past few months. Our friendship blossomed so effortlessly that I couldn't fight its natural progression. Slowly, we developed a sense of trust because he had been so steadfast. I allowed him to meet my son and when I saw how well Isaac took to him, it became clear that he was the one I should break down my guard for.

Javi and I were visiting his cousin at West Virginia University when I decided to tell him how I felt. I knew in my heart I wasn't making a mistake. The morning we arrived at the school, I told him I had feelings for him and asked if I was too late. Javi was happy to hear that. His feelings hadn't changed. His unwavering support became the foundation of our healthy relationship. We had both learned from our mistakes in previous relationships. He had been with someone for four years on and off, but now he knew what he wanted. He had goals and hobbies. There was a personality behind that handsome face.

One of the things I loved best about Javi was that his family was the center of his life.Even though I only had a few blood relatives to call my own, this was a quality that was essential to me. As my own small family was growing, Javi brought me into his. They are a large, warm, and welcoming family, who had open arms from the moment I was introduced. I wasn't accustomed to such hospitality.

Choosing to let Javi in was the best decision I had made in a very long time. We were like little torn pieces from a book. Only together would we make sense. It was like we were pushing each other in the right direction. Even the smallest of gestures showed his willingness to compromise on any level. For example, Javi had never liked animals. Now, here he was embracing my love of canines and shopping for a new dog with me. We just worked.

♦

To be honest, fighting was a part of our relationship, too. Our love for each other had been growing quickly and impossibly stronger each day. That part was perfect. But just as passionately as you can love someone, your fights can mirror that intensity. After a year together and a few months living under the same roof, Javi and I got into what I would have deemed a relatively normal fight. And, of course, *Teen Mom 2* was there to film the entire showdown.

Just like the television screen makes images seem larger than life, it magnified the incident itself. If the angles were a little deeper and the camera could see within my anxiety-ridden soul, then maybe you'd get how things escalated so quickly. The whole fight was the result of a cascade of unfortunate accidents. In the corner, our dog was shitting on the floor. I asked Javi to take him outside. It felt like there were people everywhere, invading my breathing space. I felt the walls caving in and the oxygen draining from inside the small room. The congestion in the house caused me to overreact. I lashed out and pushed Javi. He went outside to fix my car and that was it. That was probably one of our shortest fights and, thankfully, most of them are over stupid things (like the dog shitting in the corner of the room). However, lashing out at Javi wasn't okay and the incident forced me to recognize that the real source of my angry outburst needed to be addressed. I had avoided dealing with it long enough. The first thing I did was to confide to my cousins, Jen and Candy, that I was having trouble controlling my emotions. They warned me that I might have bipolar disorder. It runs in my family and deep down I have always suspected that I had it too. Bipolar disorder, also known as manic depressive disorder, is a condition in which you experience extreme mood shifts, from severe depression to manic irritability or euphoria. I knew my cousins were right because I could go from being at zero to full-throttle angry in minutes. Then, I would be fine a few minutes later. I want to be clear that being bipolar does not mean that I, or anyone else who has it, is violent. Contrary to some of the gossip and rumors that have been circulated, I am not an aggressive or violent person. I visited the doctor and the diagnosis proved my cousins' instincts were correct. I was relieved the solution was simple. Regular counseling and medications were the steps to a better me.

These dramatic events were enough to last me decades. I focused my attention on what mattered. Javi and I began planning our future together. After all, he had become my chosen family. In order to provide a future for himself and our family, he decided to join the United States Air force. He would be both serving our country and giving us stability. This noble, selfless commitment proved his loyalty not only to me, but to a greater good, something bigger than the both of us.

This career choice meant a very big change for how we would operate as a couple and, although I was proud of Javi, I was scared for what it would mean for us.

14

Girl Friends

Meanwhile, there were problems brewing from the outside from someone who I had thought cared about me. I wasn't prepared that the next crisis in my life would involve my close friend, Aria. In my opinion she had been bringing herself down by befriending strippers and changing herself to fit into her new crowd. I confronted her, making it clear that I didn't want to be around that lifestyle and we couldn't be friends if she continued to be a part of it. This fight led us to the end of our friendship and worse.

Aria and I had been friends for years. I didn't want to lose her friendship, but sometimes you have to let go of an unhealthy relationship even if it means losing something that used to be great. The issue between us quickly escalated into the biggest blowup I had ever had in my life, and by the end some old skeletons from my past had been dragged out into the public eye.

Back in middle school, I had this friend with whom I was close, very close. In fact, our friendship was blurry and experimental. We didn't have boyfriends, so we used to practice on each other. We kissed and touched each other. At such a young age, I didn't stop to analyze what this meant about my sexuality—even though I knew we had a unique friendship, and the twinges of jealousy I felt ached more than if she was just a regular friend. I'd get upset if she hung out with other friends, thinking she could be doing the same things with them. Was I just being promiscuous? I never considered myself to be gay. We hid the physical part of our relationship from her mom because we knew we were different from the other girls at school, and we had some instilled guilt that what we were doing would not be considered "acceptable." Looking back, I realize that I thought of her as my girlfriend even if we never officially acknowledged it. Years later, she came out as a lesbian.

Since then, I had only had sexual experiences with guys. Girls never crossed my mind again as an option—until Aria. To clarify my relationship with Aria: we never dated. We were never teetering between friendship and a relationship. While I was still living at Jo's, we hooked up once. This wasn't Girls Gone Wild shit. I felt an indescribable love for Aria. It wasn't romantic love, but that didn't make it any less meaningful.

There was a deleted scene from *Teen Mom 2* where we discussed the nature of our friendship and if it would ever go further. I had never really sat down to examine my sexuality, but Aria was convinced I was gay like her. I didn't want to be stereotyped as a closeted lesbian. For me it's much more complicated than that. I was happy with Javi and I felt like Aria wanted to destroy that. Maybe she thought her influence would help me be a free butterfly and declare my true sexuality to the world, but I felt like she was too intensely eager to push me towards girls. There is no denying my attraction to certain women, but in my mind there was no need for the discussion because experimentation is as far as I ever wanted to go. I honestly believe that nobody is completely straight and attraction to the same sex is natural, but Aria's insistence that I should only be with girls was not true to who I am. I felt like she kept telling me what I wanted, but really it was just what she wanted. I didn't want to be with Aria or any girl for that matter. I should have been clearer with her, but I lightly passed the discussion off with a mere shrug and a "maybe" to being open to dating women.

Instead of allowing me to make my own choices, Aria told Javi that I was gay and I would eventually leave him for a woman. Javi believed she was telling the truth because Aria was my best friend. Why would she lie? He left me without even hearing me out and went to stay with some friends at Bloomsburg University, two hours away. I panicked beyond belief and went after him. As I drove, my mind raced through several horrible scenarios. I was terrified that I was about to lose the best thing that had ever happened to me. What if right now his friends were convincing him to end it with me? I could almost hear the lesbian jokes being thrown around at my expense. I didn't need to be pigeonholed by anyone. My sexuality wasn't a joke or anyone's business.

I was hoping to have a calm discussion with Javi to explain that Aria had skewed our conversation to sound like I was interested in dating women, but I never got the chance. As soon as I arrived on campus, I was confronted by ten sorority girls, accompanied by a guy who grabbed me and prevented me from seeing Javi. He repeatedly said how awful I was and the girls pushed me around. Luckily, I had two friends with me who shoved the guy off and tried to resolve the situation. But the incident continued to escalate. It was easily the worst night of my life. I went home to cry myself to sleep, wishing the mess would disappear and still hearing their screams of *Fuck Isaac* ringing in my ears.

Although—many, many months down the road—Aria did explain to Javi that she had misrepresented the details of our conversation, in that moment, he didn't want to hear it. I was terrified he was finished with me for good. I felt like my world had been torn to shreds, leaving me alone and vulnerable. Aria was no longer my friend. Javi probably never wanted to see me again. What was I going to do now?

I waited. I hoped. As I slummed in misery, I heard Aria had sold the story she told Javi to the media. I don't know if she really did, but the tabloids had a field day. I knew the rumors would stay rumors as long as I didn't speak up, so I let the headlines slide by without comment. In no shape or form was I ashamed of my actions or who I was, but declaring myself a certain sexuality was a label that I refused to be burdened with. I wasn't going to allow the media to use me as a poster child for closeted gays. It wouldn't be fair to those who truly had such difficulty expressing who they are. Now that is a difficult journey.

Fundamentally, I knew there was one definite in my life—Javi. Thankfully, the love Javi and I possess proved to be stronger than the drama the rumors and lies had brought into our lives. Javi eventually cooled down and we were able to find a way around the anger and hurt.

The major cliché of what doesn't kill you makes you stronger applies heavily in our case. Interrogating myself under a bright light for days crystallized one fact for me: I wanted to marry Javi. Deep down I had known it all along. I didn't want to waste any more time holding back from what I truly wanted. Javi was opposed to waiting any longer, too. He would be entering the Air Force soon. We didn't want to part without calling each other husband and wife, so we decided to marry in Vegas.

We went all the way south, with the MTV camera crew in tow, but our minds changed instantly. Eloping in a dime a dozen chapel below flickering fluorescent lights, where you could choose a sci-fi theme or have a fake Elvis memento, seemed cheesy and unromantic. Once we got down there, I realized I didn't want my wedding to be like that so we decided it would be best to wait.

15

STEADFAST CONVICTIONS

Religion tends to become an issue once marriage begins to come up in conversation. Javi's family is very religious but fortunately they didn't expect us to have a church wedding. Personally, I didn't have a lot of expectations or demands for how the ceremony should be, but the one thing I have never wanted is a church wedding. I don't want to be married in a church because I do not believe in God.

How can you not believe in God? I'm sure that's what a lot of people want to ask me. For me, that question is actually easily answered. Just like some Catholics quote Bible passages to support their views, I look to the many experiences in my own life that have proved to me that there is no reason to believe.

I am not in any way susceptible to "Catholic guilt." I can't be frightened into faith by stories of the fiery pits of hell. Contrary to what some people think, atheists aren't heathens with no moral compass. In fact, most atheists base their ideas on science, facts, and hard evidence. Atheism doesn't make you less human, just a more a logical one.

I never had much interest in being part of a religious institution or community. To me, blind faith in the unknown or in an after life is just an excuse to believe in something other than yourself. My perception of the universe is more existential. I believe in myself. Why believe in what's basically an imaginary friend? There are other ways to explain the mysteries of life. I believe in science. Science can clearly debunk religious myths and provide concrete answers to what religion tries to explain through stories. I don't believe a god created the universe. I rely on the Big Bang theory to understand Creation. Science helps me comprehend life and the larger picture of how we came to be.

I suppose my scientific mind is the result of having no religious influences during my childhood. I don't remember my mom ever taking me to church or encouraging prayer. Occasionally, she told me to say a prayer before bed, but that's it. It was the classic one most people say: *Now I lay me down to sleep. I pray the Lord my soul to keep. If I should die before I wake, I pray the Lord my soul to take.* If you think about it, saying take me to heaven in case I die tonight is a pretty morbid way to end your day. I think it's a cheap way to try to get into heaven even if you weren't particularly religious or a good person in life.

The idea of living after my bones wither to nothing is more disturbing than comforting to me. Living forever, as though we are never truly put to rest, is a scary thought. A true end to our lives on earth seems more natural. I don't believe there's anything after this. From a rational, scientific perspective an afterlife makes no sense to me. I've never encountered ghosts or spirits so I have no belief in them either. Once you're dead, I believe you are gone completely. There's nothing that follows.

Looking for factual evidence to provide an alternative explanation for life is frowned upon by some people of faith. To me, there's no solid proof of God's existence. I believe the Shroud of Turin can be explained in one of two ways: either it was an elaborate hoax or there is a scientific explanation of how some guy's face became imprinted on an old rag. I know that I may sound cynical, but to be honest I'd rather turn to my dog for help than pray to a god we have no proof even exists.

For me religion creates more questions than answers. Like when people say, *Life's a test.* I've watched too many good people become engulfed in shitty situations, to find comfort in that idea. Why would a god put people through terrible things? I don't care if you're testing me. To me, that's like saying Jigsaw was definitely doing a righteous move by torturing strangers in *Saw.* I understand that for many, being part of the church is comforting. I go to the gym to obtain similar effects. Physical and spiritual all in one for the price of twenty dollars a month!

Joking aside, even though I just can't bring myself to blindly believe in an abstract being, since faith is primarily based on a being you can't see or touch, I do believe it takes guts to go on that alone. Even though I have strong opinions I try to respect other people's beliefs.

♦

My own family's history is a testament to the randomness of the universe and all the proof I need that there is no grand divine plan. Misfortune and tragedy have been a constant in our lives, passed down like toxic heirlooms from one generation to the next. Beginning with my grandparents, two of the most saintly people I'll ever know. Together, they have experienced more unjustifiable loss than anyone ever should.

My grandfather was in a car accident that resulted in an innocent death. According to my mom, he stopped on a steep hill. When he moved forward a van was speeding toward him and he couldn't stop in time to prevent a collision. He crashed into this oncoming vehicle and one of the children on board was killed. It was someone else's mistake, but he was devastated. Ultimately, the evidence proved he was not at fault, but he could not shake the guilt. There was no intent or even negligence on his part, yet in his mind he condemned himself. Can you imagine living with that?

My grandfather was never a fan of crowds and being surrounded by a ton of people, but in addition to my Aunt Jodi's death, the accident pushed him farther away from people. He shut himself off from the world. Despite all this tragedy my grandfather has remained strong. His legs were already bad from his time as a Marine, but they have deteriorated significantly as he struggles to take care of my grandmother. She's in the middle stages of Alzheimer's. Recently, she was put into a nursing home. Alzheimer's disease is a neurological disorder that causes your brain cells to die. Your memory fades. Your lover's face is no longer familiar. Love is gone. Your body wastes away to nothing. I don't want the images. I wish I could hold her hand to comfort any part of her that is still here. To me, my grandfather's strength and determination to take care of his wife in the face of such hopelessness defines faith.

Is disease a test? Is it a punishment? What did my grandmother do to deserve such a brutal disease? Still not convinced? What about miscarriages? What's the plan there? My grandmother had two of them.

Next is the death of my aunt at the hands of a drunk driver at the age of eighteen. My mother never fully recovered from the loss and I feel she has used alcohol to numb her pain ever since. Why did she have to lose her sister? If God had a plan, he would have known my mother would turn to alcohol. Ironically, her drinking is exactly what started me down the road to atheism. Was that part of the plan, too?

I have only been to church once. I don't pretend to have studied the religions of the world or to fully understand all that they embody, but I do believe that what my grandparents have endured is true faith. They have had a more powerful influence in my life than any flawed organized religion. Even at the peak of my grandfather's hermit lifestyle, he still tried to help my mother. My grandparents played a large role in raising me during middle school. Sadly, I don't have any contact with my grandparents now. From what I head from family members, my mom created a hell of a story. She accused me of stealing $10,000 from Jo and told them I was headed to jail because I was charged with a felony. In reality, I didn't do anything, but that could be the reason they cut me off.

My grandparents do not want a funeral or any mourning when they die. My fear of regret is enormous. I feel like I can't say my last goodbyes because they won't respond. If anything were to happen, I don't want to feel remorse on top of grief. I still leave voicemails every so often to update them on my life, but it sometimes feels like I am just pretending that they are still in my life. I hope they still care about me and Isaac.

These painful struggles of my family are enough reason for me to turn my back on God and religion. I'm comfortable and satisfied with my own beliefs. There's nothing anyone can say to change my view. I apologize if I have offended anyone.

Javi's family is religious. He doesn't attend church or see himself as a practicing Catholic, however, because of his upbringing our children will be baptized so they can choose what they want for themselves in the future. I don't want to impress any sort of belief system on them. Since baptism will allow Isaac the freedom of choice when he is older to remain Catholic or pursue a different vision, the choice for me was simple.

I know very well that religion and politics are controversial and contentious topics, but that is a flaw of our society. We should all strive for a higher level of tolerance. While I may not fully understand blind faith, I respect those who possess it. My grandparents are Methodists and their faith is what keeps them moving and fighting to live.

My strong views on God and religion have gotten me into trouble in the past. I've had people tell me they can't support me because I am an atheist. The religious versus the non-believers is a bit like the tattoo debate. Is atheism dangerous? Are tattoos taboo? Tattoos are generally accepted because so many people have at least one. Atheism is similar. Acceptance of either atheism or tattoos is based on openness. If you're not willing to accept the fact that I am an atheist then so be it.

16

INK INSANITY

I've always been attracted to tattoos and the people who have them. Tattoos represent who you are and your story. My latest piece is a full sleeve. I'm still working on it part by part with an artist. Right now, the inside is an anatomical heart and time bomb representing my short fuse and impatience. There are also skulls, representing the "skeletons in my closet," alongside roses. The roses represent my mother. She actually has a tattoo of roses with stretch marks from her pregnancy running through the flowers. I feel like this tattoo is really the only significant bond we've ever had. The roses represent my past with her and are a symbol of the only remaining thread connecting me to the time I was living inside her as a baby.

After Isaac was born, I needed to have some sort of tattoo for him. His name and birth date are not enough so I have dedicated my entire back to him. Since I've found an artist whose work I love, he has been helping me cover up previous work done by someone else. The piece I have now is a mess, but the part I love is the quote next to Isaac's initials: *To the world you are one person but to one person you are the world.* At the moment it is still a work in progress, but we're planning on covering up the design surrounding the quote. Hopefully I'll be gaining a very large art piece I'll be satisfied with. Definitely, a very painful procedure on the back, that's for sure.

My single piece on my thigh is a dream catcher. While I was in Texas, I found out that I have Native American blood on my father's side. Like most of my other tattoos, the dream catcher holds a double meaning. To me, it is a powerful symbol that represents both my journey of self-discovery and my determination to realize my dreams despite obstacles thrown in my path.

There are a few random ones I have alongside these bigger pieces. I used to have a puzzle piece that I decided to have removed. The mermaid along the outside of my arm is to remind me of how I should always view myself.

I'm pretty open about how I feel and I've had some hateful comments toward this art form where the body is the canvas. I hate how people say it's unattractive when girls get so many tattoos. It's more acceptable to have a star on your inner forearm or a large tramp stamp that you'll probably regret, but sleeves and larger pieces are viewed as trashy and ugly. I think tattoos make people more beautiful. It's wearing little, true pieces of the inner you on the outside for the world to see. I've had criticism from people online saying how gross it is for a girl to be covered up in tattoos. To them, it's impossible for a girl to be feminine and sexy yet love body modification. Sort of funny since guys seem to drool over Kat Von D and she obviously has quite a bit of work covering her entire body.

I might take her as my inspiration because I don't see myself stopping anytime soon. I'm finishing the sleeve I'm working on now and then the needle will find its way onto my other arm for another sleeve. Just to be a smartass, I'll have two sleeves and still have a successful career and prove all the naysayers wrong. Tattoos aren't taboo anymore. I know people who have their entire bodies covered by tattoos, yet work for major corporations in some of the top positions.

I've always been a big believer in 'if it doesn't hurt you then don't get your underwear in a knot over it.' Tattoos make me feel more complete and beautiful. It's like going in for a new haircut or buying a new wardrobe. Okay, it's a little more permanent than that. Tattoos are an extension of my motto: I'm always a work in progress.

♦

The backlash of criticism I received for my views on tattoos and religion was rough, but it was nothing compared to how I could tear myself down. I am my harshest critic. I have been obsessed with my weight since middle school. Fat was my enemy. Poor body image is something I have struggled to overcome my entire life. This issue is common among girls, but I took the obsession too far. Looking back at photos of me taken pre-Isaac, I can see that I was a healthy weight. But even back then, when I had an effortlessly thin body, I still wasn't happy. I have never felt skinny enough, ever.

Even as uncomfortable and ugly as I felt, I didn't want to change my eating habits. I was a carbaholic. I loved bread, pasta, and potatoes. Green foods were foreign and flavorless.

Fruits were okay. Eliminating carbs was like taking *Toy Story* figurines from Isaac. Don't do it! It's really not nice.

If my food choices didn't change, something else had to. The post pregnancy weight was hugging my stomach like a monkey on a tree. I tried a trainer. I tried cutting back. Refined sugar is in everything, I swear! The Chunky Monkey ice cream container staring down from the freezer racks mocked me. That was actually my mom's nickname for me. Don't most body image issues start at home? Mine did and it made me notice how all the other girls were so much daintier and petite than I was. My height always made me stick out. As a tall girl, I'm naturally going to weigh a bit more than other girls. Even though I was a healthy weight, the number on the scale seemed to matter more than the lack of fat on my body. I didn't want to weigh triple digits.

My self-esteem never matched the digits on the scale. It didn't help to have a friend who based her thinspiration on underweight models' tactics. She was bulimic and anorexic and she encouraged me to start down the same path. We were a pair of anorexic teenagers who became caught up in an unhealthy trend. Fortunately I had the sense to break the pattern while I was pregnant. Isaac needed nutrition and I wasn't stupid or selfish enough to deny food to the baby growing inside of me.

But I went back to my old habits shortly after Isaac was born. I stopped eating or opted for minimal items. I'd chew a piece of gum that's only five calories. I'd drink water to fill up my stomach. I realize now that these are stupid ways to lose weight; you end up gaining it back next week. But anorexia defies logic. You are literally starving your body of the nutrition it needs and the consequences can be deadly.

Looking for better results, my habits took an even more dangerous turn. I'd do the most intense workout devised, Insanity—a home workout DVD that is supposed to help transform your body in sixty days. I'd do a forty-five minute session and then not replenish my body with water or nutrients. Instead, I would make myself throw up. That's how desperately I wanted to be thin. Not a day went by that I didn't wish to be skinnier and to feel comfortable wearing whatever I wanted. Getting dressed in the morning should never be as difficult as I made it. I chose to wear sweatpants and leggings. Jeans were never an option. The number on the label indicating my pants size didn't read beautiful to me. Whenever I looked in the mirror, I saw a "chunky monkey" staring back at me.

Enough was enough. I decided that it was time for me to take back control of my body image. With age and maturity, I've learned that only I have the power to make myself feel good. I am the only one who can change my attitude towards my body. To boost my self-esteem and hopefully help others who have similar issues, I agreed to do a photo shoot for a campaign called, "Beauty is Sizeless." The photographer, Katie Hedrick, contacted me and explained the project's purpose of teaching others to value themselves in every way possible. She made me feel comfortable and empowered as she photographed me in a bright blue Betsey Johnson dress. Having my makeup and hair done brought out the confidence buried within. I decided to strive to keep this as my attitude on an everyday basis. A few months later we had chosen a specific shot. A black and white, soft light, flattering shot of me clad in a bra and jeans. I was wearing jeans and proud of my body, damn it! My quote on the photo reflected how I finally felt about myself. It said:

> *The definition of true beauty is being a hundred percent comfortable in your own skin. It's having confidence in yourself even if you don't meet the standards of how others expect you to look. True beauty is the ability to love yourself and all the flaws you come with. When you love and respect yourself and wear your confidence, everyone else will see it.*

Size zero skinny jeans may not be hugging my hips anytime soon, but I no longer feel ashamed of my body. True beauty comes from within and being healthy is so much more important than the size you wear.

Beauty Is Sizeless campaign.

17

The Three Rings of Marriage

He passed! He passed! He passed! Flying colors and all, Javi passed the ASVB (Armed Services Vocational Aptitude Battery), the initial required test to enter the United States Air Force. The overwhelming excitement and sense of pride I felt were paired with a hollowed-out pit in my stomach. Training camp in Texas was less than six months away so pushing the sadness down was like pretending Brussels sprouts were Snickers bars.

Tough times were ahead, but we tried not to dwell on it. There'd be plenty of lonely days and nights for me to sulk. Since Javi would be leaving for basic training so soon, we agreed to put our marriage plans on hold. I had already decided that I wanted to go through the normal steps and get engaged, not just hitch up quickly and quietly. But even if we couldn't get married yet, we still had plenty to celebrate and be thankful for. Javi's career path was lining up neatly.

A celebratory dinner out was in order. Early one day, a few weeks later, Javi took Isaac out and I sensed a devious, secret strategy being carried out by my two boys. I had no idea what they were up to, but obliged their request to keep their surprise a surprise. Later, I drove by myself to Honesdale, the town I grew up in, to meet them. Javi had chosen a restaurant very close to where my old house stood, which indicated nostalgia was important to our dinner. Javi was making this very special for me, even though the dinner was meant to be a celebration of his achievement.

The mysterious instructions he'd left at home led me from Whitehall to this restaurant and up to the hostess. She handed me a cute scavenger hunt-like note:

> *Almost found us. Walk out of the restaurant. Make a right. Go down to the steps and follow the path down to the lake. Hurry. We miss you.*
>
> *Your boys,*
>
> *Jav and Isaac.*

Isaac and Javi were exactly where they said they'd be, by the scenic Lake Wallenpaupack. They were clad in ties and each holding a bouquet of flowers. The gorgeous view and their gentlemanly attire pointed to a momentous occasion. What was happening? I had thought the three of us were out to celebrate Javi. His shaky smile indicated he was nervous and that made me nervous, too. I took Javi's extended hands and listened to what he had to say,

"Well, the real reason why I brought you out here is because this was your childhood. You were raised here. I felt like this was a part of your life I wasn't part of. So I figured if I came out here, I felt like someway I would be part of it forever because you are my present now. What I really want to know now . . ." he knelt down on one knee, "is if you'll marry me."

The ecstatic electricity running through my core made responding a challenge. I nodded enthusiastically, squealing, "Of course!" Wow. Wow. Wow. He proposed! I was engaged! What? I was both stunned and exhilarated. The hugs, kisses, and tears expressed our emotions because we were too overwhelmed to speak.

The practical part came to the conversation as we settled down to our dinner. We weren't engaged for me to just stare at the beautiful, shiny "Britney Spears inspired" ring. Javi's obvious dedication to Isaac and me had been declared. Even as he prepared to leave for training, we had no question in our minds what the next step was. We wanted to be hearing wedding bells as soon as possible. Javi did me justice by following tradition and proposing to me in such a meaningful and romantic way. Looking back at Vegas, it was such a fleeting thought that seemed forever ago. The teetering back and forth had answered our questions. We were hesitant about eloping but now we were ready to start planning our wedding.

Meanwhile, life was coming at us full speed and the days were counting down as Javi prepped for Texas. There was no time to plan a big ceremony, so we decided to go to the courthouse to get the legal formalities out of the way. Since I am an atheist, we had already agreed not to have a church ceremony and to focus on planning a big wedding celebration in the future.

As joyful as I was to be getting married, truthfully I was a little disappointed that the ceremony would be happening in a courthouse. It all felt so matter of fact and unmagical.

Every couple has to sign papers to get a marriage license, but this meant something a little different to me. Since the time constraint and our financial resources meant that I couldn't have my dream wedding ceremony, I desperately wanted to turn the simplistic, legal rite into a special day.

In retrospect, the experience surpassed my expectations of the day. The courthouse ritual was unexpectedly emotional and meaningful, despite my wanting a larger ceremony. I was crying like a baby as I said my vows because I knew, beyond a shadow of a doubt, that we were meant to be together. There wasn't a bone, muscle, or ligament in my body telling me the moment was wrong. Any onlooker could tell what I was feeling inside. It felt so right.

Even though getting married at the courthouse wasn't romantic, especially as dozens of people were also there to file for divorce, Javi and I were properly dressed for the occasion. I wore a simple, lacy ivory dress while Javi and Isaac had on button-downs and dress pants. Javi had his mother and Miguel, a good friend, to stand in as witnesses. The judge read a passage out of the Bible, which I wasn't happy about, but I decided to overlook it and focus on the vows we were told to repeat. Then, all of a sudden, we were officially married. That was it. The huge wedding–with dancing, cake, and champagne—that I wanted would hopefully be reserved for the fall. After all, Javi and I still wanted to celebrate our marriage with those who loved us most. On the other hand, love doesn't wait for life's schedule to open up.

There was one person I was worried wouldn't take the news of our engagement quite so well. I hadn't told Jo yet and I would have to explain what this would mean for him and Isaac. We had been getting along relatively well, but I was guessing any content period we'd had was inching toward the drain. In fact, Jo would probably full out hate me for what I was about to tell him.

Javi's military base placement would be somewhere other than Pennsylvania, which meant we could be moving a remarkable distance. Javi and had I made a commitment to one another, and Isaac and I would follow him wherever he was stationed. This obviously could have a huge impact on Jo's relationship with Isaac. It was never my intention to take my son from his father, but in the long haul I knew this was the best option for Isaac and me. Javi undeniably loved Isaac and viewed him as a son. My mind was one hundred percent set.

For such a significant decision, I knew Jo needed to be informed immediately. Our ability to maintain a civil adult relationship as Isaac's parents would depend on how we handled this situation. Communication was the solution, per co-parenting counseling advice. I wasn't just going through the motions to be polite, though. I genuinely care about Jo's feelings when it comes to Isaac.

Jo, like I predicted, took my marriage as a sham. He argued that I had rushed into a serious commitment that I was surely not ready for. Javi and I almost had a year together, which wasn't acceptable to Jo, but to me the number held less significance than the depth of our feelings. I hadn't been impulsive with such a huge decision. Javi and I weren't a joke. Jo's inability, at the time, to see the real reason why Javi and I chose to get married excused his poor judgment in sizing us up. I think Jo doubted my relationship with Javi because he wasn't sure what he wanted and saw Javi as the ultimate barricade to ever having "us" as a possibility again.

Jo's reaction exceeded my low expectations, in that he didn't throw a fit or threaten to take me to court (although there would be plenty of that in our future). Custody has always been a struggle for us. We need to learn to work together to divide up time in order for Isaac to see both of us. Co-parenting means working together to meet Isaac's needs, no matter what compromises and sacrifices we have to make. In order for me to move with Isaac, we would need to readjust the custody agreement. I was willing to work to find a way to give Jo the time he needed. Christmas? Major holidays? Summers? The judge, hopefully, would comprehend the move wasn't whimsical wanderlust. It was an opportunity for me to provide a whole, stable family.

Co-parenting is doable knowing that we are all so much better off than if Jo and I had stayed together. It's not like I dread dropping off Isaac at Jo's. Of course, I wish I could have Isaac all of the time, but the way we live now is a hundred times better than how I picture us living if Jo and I had stayed together. Harmoniously co-parenting Isaac has taken some transitioning to get used to. There were plenty of fights over allotted time slots when we each could have Isaac, many of which have had to be resolved in court.

Isaac loves Javi. He also loves Jo and knows that he is his father. Despite the many fights and the anger I have felt over the years, I do my best not to let Isaac hear me say anything negative about his father. Jo and I have our own issues, but keeping our son out of it is essential to protecting him from our mistakes. Isaac's happiness is so much more important than anything else that's going on. In the beginning, I really believed Isaac's happiness was solely dependent on Jo and me working out our kinks. Now I realize we are so much healthier giving Isaac two whole families that love him unconditionally.

♦

The most difficult part of co-parenting is that you are still in each other's lives and sometimes it's a challenge to totally stay out. While I may have been seen as the one who wanted to make our family work, for a long time Jo felt the same way, too. I've lost count of all the times he's wanted to hook up with me. He did succeed when I was at my most vulnerable, in terms of my feelings for him, and I had lost a very important person in my life, Jordan, because of it. In between relationships, when Javi and I weren't together, I did hook up with Jo. I had made the same mistake over and over. I've learned though. Jo continued to pursue me but I was done trying to convince myself that he wanted more than just hook ups. I would never cheat ever again. Javi means too much to me.

Jo's girlfriend was the problem for me now. I had no jealousy or hatred for his new girlfriend, only anger. He had started seeing a girl who I suspected might be a pot smoker. I hadn't smoked weed since I got pregnant with Isaac and it is something I no longer want in our lives. I had expected others would respect that I did not want my son to be around mind-altering substances. People change under the influence and I would never trust anyone I don't know personally who's high or drunk. Smoking weed and underage drinking is a personal choice. While I never saw her smoke pot myself, and Jo denied that she did, her social media content seemed to boast her high life choices.

The trouble started at the snap of a photo a few months into their relationship. Her apparent lack of discretion turned heads, including mine. She posted pictures online of herself wearing a gas mask and smoking out of what looked like a bong. It seemed this was beyond an anxiety reducing, self-medicating pastime. I was afraid it was a bad habit my son could potentially pick up one day. There was no way I wanted

Isaac to be around weed or alcohol. I understood the full, detrimental repercussions. All I asked of Jo was that he keep Isaac away from it.

Thanks to the girl's need to incessantly update her social media, I read posts that led me to believe she might be drinking around Isaac and that she may have been drinking with Jo's dad during Jo's weekend to have Isaac. I was furious. If true, there was nothing I could do about the situation, but I didn't want her around my son.

The backlash I received for my feelings, infuriated me more than typical hate mail. I'm not the girl who buys into the old "everybody does it" cliché, so my disapproval for underage drinking isn't all that surprising. You can't have it all. You can't partake in the merry idiocy and be in a relationship with someone who has a bigger priority than partying. Isaac is a priority in Jo's life, too. I've never pretended to know every little detail about this girl or her relationship with Jo, but I felt her social media posts hinted at childish and stupid behavior.

I tolerated the idea of her in the beginning, even though the stupid stepmother notion caused some strain on my heart. Isaac was my baby. I didn't want to be replaced by this girl.But, I quickly realized I will always hold a special place in Isaac's life. Always. She never will.

How quickly my thoughts jump from her to my son. He is always at the forefront, the epicenter of my universe. That's what all the people sending me hate failed to understand. Jo's girlfriend never mattered to me. She still doesn't. It's my son. He is the prime source in my life that love springs from. There was no showdown or bitch slapping over Jo. Please.

I'm not jealous. The Jo of my life was over long ago. I've given up on providing Isaac with two parents who are together yet miserable. Javi is the one who completes my true family. But the reality is that Jo will be in my life forever and for the immediate future so will his girlfriend. She will never see where I'm coming from, and I'd rather not waste any more breath trying to explain why I can't pretend to like her or reason with her. It's done. I'll always be the bad person. I'll always be the bitter ex.

Javi and I get married at the courthouse in Salisbury, PA.

18

AIRMAN MARROQUIN

As Javi left for three months of training at Lackland Air Force Base in San Antonio, Texas, I was left at home feeling more alone than ever. The hole I felt without him grew bigger each day. Thankfully, Javi's family was there to support me and help keep me sane. His sister, Lidia, persistently offered help with Isaac, which reminded me I was never truly alone. Javi's brother, Sal, became a person I learned to trust and love. He became like a brother to me and we spent almost every day together. I never really understood the source of strength family bonds could provide until I was absorbed into Javi's.

However, the nights where I turned to face his empty side of the bed were still full of loneliness. There was a cold emptiness where pillows lined up in place of the warm body that should have been there. Nobody could really fill that hole because I only wanted him. Since it was policy for no phone calls in the first few weeks of training, I scribbled on plenty of paper, sending out letters of love to temporarily close up the gaping hole. There was a sense of romance behind writing letters, as if we weren't living in the age of social media and to-the-minute updates on what we just ate or where we plan on going next, but the downside to writing letters is how quickly outdated everything you have written becomes. No matter how much or how frequently I wrote to Javi, I couldn't keep him in the loop.

The lack of daily communication was heart wrenching. Being in a relationship is all about communication. At that point, my marriage had none. It wasn't anyone's fault, but the separation was proving to be more of a challenge than I had originally thought it would be. For our generation, cell phones are like extra limbs. Texting and calling is second nature. I constantly had to resist habitually typing Javi's name into my phone to send him a few quick words. It was all so abnormal in the beginning.

Thankfully, a few weeks in, phone conversations were allowed and the five-minute call we were granted every two weeks was precious, like an overdue paycheck you had been working so hard for. Commercials last longer than the conversations we were allowed to have. The effort to fit every syllable into those few minutes was rushed and desperate. Thankfully Javi couldn't see me because I sometimes felt my rapid mouth movements and drastic hand gestures made me look like a used car salesman. We made these crazy, long distance phone calls work as best as possible.

While Javi and I were making it through on the little communication we had, I couldn't help but roll my eyes at girls who cried over not seeing their boyfriends for a day or two. Try going months and never seeing his face. Not having the one loyal person who loved me and made me the happiest girl around, taught me the value of a simple call or even to have a night in with your loved one. It made me resort back to everything I was used to when I had been surviving solo. How I fared on my own reminded me that I did have the strength to keep going.

The five-minute phone calls were never as satisfying as I hoped they would be. Really they were just a reminder of my loneliness. At some point, they stopped being helpful at all and I completely lost it. For two days I questioned why I had chosen to put myself through such torture. I was young, but I was also a mother. Why didn't I choose someone who would be able to be around? Being in a long distance relationship was a test I had never taken. So far, I felt like I was totally failing. I wasn't just questioning a relationship but a marriage and I wasn't sure how to find the answers I needed. I wanted to be done with the separation. I wanted to have Javi with me, but that was not an option at all. Discussing the marriage or how difficult the situation was for me wasn't possible either. The crisis was mine alone to deal with.

Thankfully, Sal, Javi's brother, was there to help me sort it all out. He dealt it up straight to me, reminding me of all of the reasons why I was married to a man living over a thousand miles away from me. It wasn't ridiculous. The sacrifice made all the sense in the world when I heard it from someone else. I just needed reminding. The love hadn't disappeared. Javi wasn't here but the feelings were still strong. I just needed a little bit of a push to keep me going to the end.

The phone conversations became more frequent towards the end of his training. I had more access to Javi, including nights and weekends—almost like an advertisement from a phone company. *Free nights and weekends, y'all!* Their instructor allowed a weekly ten-minute phone call as long as they didn't mess up severely. I wasn't able to hug him or kiss him, but I was so excited to be gaining more of Javi back. The timing of the calls sucked, though. I'd usually be elbow-deep in bubbles, bathing Isaac, or in the middle of making dinner during the time Javi could speak to me. I'd become so engrossed in what we were talking about that I'd burn the chicken. Even when I could focus on our conversation, sometimes we were just out of step with one another. He was living one way now and I was still living the same way we were before he left.

I was lucky to have great friends to keep me busy until the days crept up to Javi's graduation. It was the day we were all so proud and excited to finally reach. All of Javi's hard work had paid off and he was joining a prestigious rank of honor to serve our country's military. The nobility behind that sacrifice took a courage I couldn't match up to. I was so excited to be going back down to Texas, not only to see my family, but also to be reunited with my husband. It was the most built up anticipation I had ever endured.

Leading up to the day I left for Texas, Jo sat me down to talk. We weren't having many heart-to-hearts recently, so I was a little shocked to hear that he wanted to talk about more than just what Isaac did that day. I was a little uncomfortable as Jo began to express his true feelings. "I want my family back," he said defiantly.

Pre-Jordan, I had wanted us to be a family so badly. I had cried. I had whined. It seemed like the only way to be happy at the time. But I was so wrong.

Jo went on to say he couldn't sleep straight for a year. I almost gasped at the serious tone his voice had taken on. As he spoke, I couldn't help but notice he didn't mention his girlfriend once. He didn't even acknowledge the fact that he wasn't single. Why? I think she had no idea what his true feelings were because he kept them buried deep. He never admitted any of this on television. I think Jo didn't want to reveal his wants on camera because he didn't want his girlfriend to find out. Was he trying to cover his ground without having to lose anything . . . anyone?

His honesty was real, though. Jo wanted the three of us to be together again, but I had been done with this notion for a while. It wasn't realistic. It wasn't what made me happy. We didn't work. The manner in which he presented the idea, made me feel like Jo didn't take my marriage seriously and that he failed to see it was the world to me, not some temporary situation. I was so taken aback, I didn't know what to say. All I could muster was, "I'm sorry you feel that way, Jo."

I wasn't angry with him for him approaching me in a somewhat inappropriate manner, but I was annoyed that he seemed to be hiding his feelings in order to keep his girlfriend. I was also uncomfortable because I didn't know how to respond without coming off insensitive. The idea was so weird. Jo didn't hate me? His true feelings for the past year hadn't been reflected in his actions. It was hard for me to wrap my mind around the fact he was saying he really wanted us to work and that our past hook ups weren't just physical.

Jo's demeanor toward Javi made more sense than ever. He may have approved of Jordan for whatever reason, but Javi had made a serious commitment to me and I think Jo didn't like Javi because deep down he knew that. Jo had asked me to marry him, but had never made any attempt to follow through on our engagement. It felt like just because Jo never married me, he now doubted my marriage to Javi.

Jo's words were weird, but it didn't change anything. Marriage is serious to me. I wouldn't have gone months and months without Javi if I didn't plan on seriously staying in a committed, legal bond to him. The distance had tested our love and we had passed. In my eyes, we had done more than just okay. I'd say we get a solid A for effort. Our reward was graduation day.

A few weeks later, in February of 2013, I returned to Texas to witness the United States Air Force Basic Military Training graduation ceremony. At the crack of dawn that morning, I was putting on makeup and fixing my hair. Knowing I would be seeing my husband for the first time in three months, I wanted to look as pretty as possible. My excitement was difficult to contain and my crooked eyeliner betrayed the fact that I couldn't stop my hands from trembling.

As the sun was rising, traffic built up on the interstate. Everyone was headed to the same place. Families and friends had to arrive early in order to gain a seat and not be backed up behind the thousands of cars getting their road rage on. We had to wait for hours for the ceremony to start. My leg bounced up and down nervously as everyone settled down.

The quiet breeze gave a solemn air to the ceremony. For a few brief hours I was given a glimpse of the strict, disciplined lifestyle Javi had been leading. It was overwhelming and stressful to imagine the self-discipline one needed to get through military training. I had never been more proud. Seeing the airmen and women in a sea of blue standing so still, in perfectly uniformed lines, I understood the remarkable determination that was required to be part of the military. The flag waving majestically, each ripple representing a freedom, lifted my spirits. The whole scene made you question your own patriotism and ability to live up to being a true American. The thousand graduates below us had made the ultimate sacrifice to serve our country and protect our freedoms.

I wanted to thank each and every one of them for making such a huge sacrifice, but more importantly, there was one particular graduate I wanted to see so badly. The ceremony was glorious and a little too long. We were anxiously waiting to greet the man of the hour. Every single person in the stands searched for their loved one. There was a rule: the airmen and women couldn't move from their spot until someone "tapped them out." You had to approach your loved one and tap them on the shoulder. This provided a more orderly way to join the men and women with their families. It was a little like the game Duck, Duck, Goose. But where was my goose? I scanned the rows of young men and women—their uniforms and similar haircuts making it feel like a real life version of *Where's Waldo?*—passing uniform after uniform, face after solemn face, with still no sign of Javi.

Many families had already "tapped out" their loved one. I wanted to be feeling the same joy they were experiencing. Hoping that the next face I looked at would be Javi's, my entire body shook with excitement. The hunt finally ended when Javi's face stood out like a flower among thorns. He looked so handsome in his uniform and so very different from three months ago. His face was clean-shaven and he barely had any hair on his head. I also immediately noticed that he'd lost a significant amount of weight.

I pelted myself into his arms, assuming that would count as "tapping" him out.

His family had their cameras out, snapping as many photos as possible in the initial minutes of the reunion. It felt like we were recreating those famous photographs of women seeing

At Javi's BMT graduation, February, 2013.

their military men for the first time in months. Kissing a man in uniform is a wonderful thing and then, when you cry all over their pressed blues, it ruins the formality of a momentous occasion. Just kidding.

Our reunion was so much better than what was documented in the media. The facts were straight, but the reports couldn't convey the intensity of the moment. Isaac's laughter was so joyous and adorable; happiness was nearly exploding from everyone. The newness of marriage and our relationship was coming to life again. To see Javi's face instead of just hearing his voice was so strange after all that time apart. I could hold his hand and kiss him as many times as I wanted. I didn't have to dream about it or wish it. Magical moments are rare and for a long time I didn't believe in them. Seeing Javi again created a firework display background and a soaring heart. It made me a believer again.

At Javi's graduation in Lackland, TX, with my friend Kim, cousin Kaylie, and half sister Mikaila.

19

FOR THE LOVE OF A DAUGHTER

I grew up among the wreckage of a dysfunctional family. This forced me to learn to live with disappointment and desertion. My personal search to make peace with my childhood became a journey in which I ultimately decided it was no longer healthy for me to have my parents in my life.

For years I lived in a state of denial. I wanted to believe that one day they would accept responsibility for not being the parents I felt I needed them to be. The one-sided exertion often led me to lose control of my actions and emotions. Sometimes the sad truth is forgiveness and fortitude can't salvage a relationship, even if it's with your own flesh and blood. Once I gave into that sad truth, I could no longer deny the inevitable.

I'm mature enough to realize that there are people out there who have had unbearably sad childhoods. I'm not trying to make my situation sound any worse than it actually is. I can't dumb down what has happened to me, but I also can't become a stereotypical, angry teen who allows herself to be defined by her dysfunctional, destructive past. For what I did have, I'm thankful because I remind myself of those who have it so much worse. There are kids who get beat on a regular basis. There are kids whose parents don't provide for them and so they starve. Even the most sickening situation of all, sexual assault, is something some children experience at horrifically young ages.

The darkness of some childhoods is unimaginable. Nobody wants to think about the fact that children are victimized all the time. I believe the reason this is so common is simple: not every female is meant to be a mother and not every male is meant to be a father. I've made my peace with that.

♦

It had been two years since I had flown to Texas to meet my biological father, Raymond, and even though that was the extent of our relationship, he did contact me one other time after his brother had randomly messaged me through the Internet. Since nobody had spoken to him in years, I didn't really see how he was relevant to me. It's interesting how I only started receiving these messages once I was on TV. He didn't seem to have a real reason to be contacting me either. That's when Raymond stepped in. He emailed me to apologize for his brother and told me he'd take care of it, but I'm not so naïve as to jump on these family "opportunities," with their extremely delayed timing. Raymond wasn't like his brother though. After that, he made no effort to contact me again whatsoever. I could have tap danced on the moon and learned how to breathe underwater, but it seemed like nothing was impressive enough to capture his attention for the long run.

My dad and I were done. I feel like he was never really my father anyway. I don't think of him as much more than a sperm donor. The painful memory of the one time we spent together has been memorialized on television, courtesy of MTV. It's okay, though. Meeting my sperm donor was all part of satisfying my natural curiosity. That curiosity died once I realized I wasn't meant to have a father figure in my life. He wasn't around for seventeen years of my life and I couldn't expect him to change because of one visit. I can honestly say that I am okay with not having a father in my life. It's probably one of the first times I can say that and really mean it.

Meeting my sperm donor answered all of the questions I had stacked up in mental lists for over a decade or so. Finally seeing him with my own eyes, rather than clinging to the illusion I had created, was a kind of gift in itself. There were no more made up, fake parts to my dad. The stories I had conjured up to fit in for the moments I needed a father were gone. I had a clear, solid image of who he was physically and mentally. I finally had closure.

I have grown so much because of the inescapably harsh truth. I'm so much stronger because of these toughening experiences. I feel like my mom wasn't there to rub my back and tell me how much she loved me. I don't remember her ever telling me that I *was* worth a damn when my dad sat back and didn't contact me after meeting him back when I was a frightened pregnant teenager. In my opinion, she was a "told you so" kind of mom and always would be. My mom may have been physically closer to me than my sperm donor, but she still seemed as clueless as he was.

Our current "relationship" isn't far off from what has been shown on television. It just proves we never grow. Again, I'm fine with that too. To keep myself from getting hurt, I have told my mom that we would no longer have a relationship. As a teenager, I confronted her several times. I wanted to be up front so she knew where she stood in my future.

"You will never know your grandchildren," I said spitefully, wanting to induce the same wounded feelings she raised out of me.

"I will not attend your funeral."

That seemed a bit much, even for me. What's worse than not attending your mother's memorial? I wanted to show her how intensely hurt I am and that I wasn't going to let her crawl back any time she decided she wanted to be part of my life for a split second.

I distanced myself for protection. At some point, for my own sanity, I admitted her faults to myself. After that, for years, I was consumed by anger. This was followed by the maturity to confront my demons and let go of the past. Endless tears and much counseling later, I have finally accepted what I feel is the unavoidable truth: my mother will never ever change. I no longer believe she possesses the capacity. Didn't she have a good enough reason to make the change? I guess I wasn't enough. Sure, that stings worse than a hundred bee stings, but sometimes you have to force-feed yourself the truth. It's easier to swallow down the road.

The little pieces of wisdom I have gained over the years don't make me an expert on anything, but I do believe that others can benefit from what I have learned. I have educated myself about addiction and addicts because I lived with one for a majority of my life. I wanted to learn everything I could about addiction because I wanted to understand why my mom was like this. As a child, I was confused. As a teenager, I was angry. Now, as an adult, I need answers.

When I was a teen, I recall my mother trying to get help but it seemed like she was not able to stop drinking. The nine months when I felt she was sober held so many beautiful possibilities and made me feel like life could be so wondrous. I felt myself wanting to be around her more. Sadly, I only felt this way for a short time.

I don't want my mom in my life until I feel she's accepted responsibility for how I've seen her behave. It hasn't exactly been easy for me to block her out completely, but now that she doesn't contact me very often, I've found keeping her out to be much more manageable. I will always gladly speak to her if I feel she hasn't been drinking, but if I hear the slightest bit of a slur, I will set the phone down. I have a choice now.

Every day I struggle to find forgiveness. I try to convince myself that my mother did the best job she could raising me. Do I fully believe that? No, not really. Forgiveness does not come easily. As a mother, I'd do anything for Isaac. I'd make any sacrifice to provide him with the best life possible. I believe that's what being a parent is all about—putting your child before yourself. I don't feel like my mother or father ever did that for me.

I feel like they taught me a huge parental lesson: what kind of parent *not* to be. It's like a handbook of rules and regulations type of thing. *101 Ways You Shouldn't Treat Your Child. 1,000 Situations You Should Never Put Your Child in.* So that's it. There's no magical, happy ending to my relationship or lack thereof with my parents. I don't expect anything to change. There's no more wishing for improvements.

I've found what I was looking for. Javi and his family have embraced me as one of their own. The special place I've received as an honorary member of their circle is enough for me. Everybody has problems, but how bad would it be to go through them with people like this to support you? Once in a while, I'll have a silent awareness of the big love I feel I missed out on for so long. I'll see how lovingly they treat one another, and the envy I try so hard to suppress rises up to remind me of what I wish I had.

Obviously, I feel like I come from an unhealthy place, but the love and support of the friends I've picked up over the years have salvaged my perspective on what family means. I am thankful for those who have stuck by me. On my mother's side, my cousins, Jen and Candy, have always done what's best for me. They were the same ones who went out of their way to buy me the beautiful, unique prom dress that I wore on the night Isaac was conceived. They had helped me look into adoption options when I was pregnant and still unsure if I was capable of being a mother to my baby. I am so grateful to them. Unfortunately, they both live hours away in opposite directions so we don't see each other as often as we'd like, but it's okay because I know they're only a phone call away if I do need them.

I try not to dwell on my past. I don't let my mind take me on adventures to pity land, where I'm alone and unloved. Self-pity is easy. I would know. I spent the majority of my life asking the same question: *why me?* Eventually, I realized there is always room for growth. Moving on from the past and working to improve your situation is the real challenge. Talking through my insecurities and childhood nightmares has changed the way I perceive everything. Instead of wallowing in pain and regret, I have risen from the ashes of my past. Because of that I am now stronger and healthier for myself and everyone around me. Pride over pity is the only way to live.

Isaac and Javi are my source of love and compassion. Unseen on television, Javi's family have been my rock. They have been so supportive. They warmly welcomed Isaac and me into their fold and treat us like their own. It's nice to have people to rely on if need be. I felt myself opening up and really trusting them, unlike the relationship I had with Jo's family.

Before you boo or hiss me, I am eternally grateful for every expense Jo's parents made for Isaac and me. They were so understanding and helpful during one of the toughest points in my life. They provided a roof over my head and supported me financially in so many ways. I could never express my thanks enough. If it wasn't for them, I know I wouldn't have been able to lift myself up from the ground to work my way up to where I am now. My gratitude can't be expressed.

The major issue I always had with Jo's family was the fact that our relationship felt to me like a family project. Our arguments always seemed to be a communal experience. Sometimes I felt like Jo's parents acted as barriers and referees to our fights. I know that they were just trying to protect us, but fights are frustrating enough for two people. Throw in a few more and there are just more mouths yelling.

With Javi's family it has been the opposite. They stand by us through thick and thin, but they won't take sides or involve themselves in our fights. They know there are boundaries and they try to give us a healthy space to work out our issues on our own. They don't try to push their values and feelings onto the situation, whatever it may be. Finally, my greatest desire—to be loved unconditionally—has been met with Javi and Isaac.

20

Psycho Bitch

Everything about me has been fair game for public scrutiny these past few years—my atheism, my sexuality, my motherhood, and all of my relationships. Why not bring my mental health into the public realm, too? The intrusion could have resulted in a cosmic meltdown on my part. However, I didn't explode or find myself in a predicament I couldn't figure a way out of. Instead, I confronted the major asteroids in my own galaxy by accepting my disorder and taking care of it.

My temper has risen out of the ashes on many occasions. Whenever someone provoked me, and even sometimes for no reason at all, my emotional response was instinctively anger. I'd lash out quickly and then cry. These sudden emotional strikes terrified me. My temper was an obvious trigger to relationship problems. Arguments are a normal part of any relationship. I just needed to learn not to react so emotionally. With my diagnosis, I finally had answers. It has helped me to understand the source of my violent mood swings. My temper had tainted relationships, yet I always just left it at that. I never knew my reactions added up to something as serious as bipolar disorder. I confronted it by seeking counseling, and taking the medications I need.

Unfortunately, just like all of my other personal problems, this one found its way into the gossip sites. I didn't want this to be talked about. I felt like it should be respected as something private. Do you watch people go to the bathroom or take a shower? No? Well, how is this any different? The only way anyone should know is if they snooped around in my medicine cabinet, but unfortunately it was partially my fault that my disorder became public knowledge. Someone on Twitter had been relentlessly bothering me about my mood swings and I made the mistake of responding to their badgering. It was easily figured out from there that my mood swings were symptoms of a larger problem.

I consider myself to be pretty open to the public. I just wanted this one break. I was only starting to understand my disorder and now I had others jumping down my throat online. The name-calling started. Thanks to the magic of social media, I had people calling me bipolar even before I was diagnosed. Yeah, I have some anger issues and crazy mood swings. I'm not crazy, though. Bipolar doesn't mean you're an insane person who talks to themselves and hides in the garbage. It sucks so hard that there are so many negative connotations attached to the disorder. I'm not a danger to you or to myself. I just wish the term "bipolar" wasn't so casually thrown around.

Unfortunately, I've opened myself up to criticism concerning my anger problems and even those issues concerning Jo. Although I prefer to keep my therapy sessions private, like everyone else, I did decide to let cameras come into a session Jo and I had together for co-parenting one time. This decision was purely based on the hope that by viewing us going through counseling it might help others to resolve their own conflicts in a healthy way. I have no regrets that I allowed viewers to see something real.

The problem for me is the way I've been depicted by others. Ugly and crazy are words people seem to like to associate with me. Having so many people tell you something about yourself can make you sort of believe it for a split second. As I dealt with being bipolar and going through therapy sessions, I had to also make sure negative public opinion didn't impact the way I perceived myself. These harsh ideas about the way I looked and acted had always floated in my head, but they really sprung to the forefront as others commented on them. I heard the grimy words of criticism as if they were the truth.

It's frustrating how a few moments on television can define who you are to the world. Many people have said I come off cold-hearted, crazy, psycho, bitchy, selfish—the list could take up a whole chapter. To that crowd, I am fictional. I might come off as a cold bitch but that's a classic defense mechanism for those who have been through traumatic experiences. I'm tough because I have to be. That doesn't make me crazy or a bitch. It is very strange how I went from being myself to becoming a character on television. That person sometimes seems as unreal to me as Harry Potter.

I guess that's television, though. It's segmented and two-dimensional. What can you expect? For better or worse, MTV has documented my journey of growth. These snippets have created an indelible image of who I am in the public's mind. *Teen Mom 2* viewers have either stood by solidly or bashed me relentlessly on my progress as a person. These life stages usually aren't documented and broadcast on television so excuse me if I've made mistakes along my path. I'm not bitter. Despite the dreadful times I've dealt with, I'm thankful that, in addition to the negativity and the bad reputation I may have picked up along the way, there has also been a lot of positive feedback.

There are so many people out there who can relate to the way I've reacted and handled high-pressure situations. Knowing others feel the same and that I have helped them is very comforting to me and has made the ride worth it. It's nice to have comments that are not only supportive but also understanding. It helps to reinforce the idea that the hateful comments are not indicative of who I am. It would be easy to say that I don't care. But I do. Anyone can pretend the hurtful comments don't faze them, but I won't.

Watching an episode of *Teen Mom 2* doesn't mean you know who I am or what I'm going through. Only the girls who are on the show can understand how challenging it is to put yourself and your story out to the world. Being teen mothers alone has turned us into objects of ridicule. Disapproval of us has stemmed from every facet of the media. People throwing in their negative opinions makes my blood boil. They act as if the show begs for criticism of us. *Teen Mom 2* became this huge sensation and I wasn't prepared for it. It's pure insanity if you think about it.

Despite how much criticism I've received, I'm also incredibly thankful to have had the opportunity to share my story and help others. Four seasons of *Teen Mom 2* have run through a large chunk of my life. Becoming someone recognizable on the street has been a crazy ride. I didn't do it for fame or money. I can say that a hundred times and it wouldn't make the statement more legitimate for the non-believers. Being on television has not inflated my ego. It has given me a chance to reflect on my decisions. The experience has been enlightening. It has helped me to strive to learn from my poor choices and make wiser ones in the future.

Season 1 was the beginning of the sensation that the show created. I didn't expect people to become so invested in the show since the first cast of *Teen Mom* was so heavily adored. I had to get used to the spotlight that was shining more frequently on me. Season 2 was difficult because I was so depressed. Filming was hard because I felt like shit and some viewers were becoming very vocal in their criticism of me. It deflated my spirit when I had to deal with that negativity on top of my own self-criticism.

If I made a bad choice and it was caught on film, I was sure to expect a backlash. *Why did you do that, Kail? Are you stupid? Why are you so crazy?* I didn't want to start getting so defensive online and answer the monsters. I had to grow tougher skin so I could learn to fight back in a positive way. I couldn't let the negative outweigh the positive.

Being on *Teen Mom 2* is like having home videos on a major television network. I wasn't frantically grabbing for a video camera or my phone to capture first moments or a birthday. Of course I documented these moments myself, but I also knew I had professionals doing it. Hopefully, some day when Isaac is older and watches the show he will see my constant, thriving need for pride over pity. He's already impressed by his cameos, so wait until he comprehends things more. The show is very sentimental and special to me in that sense.

I'm glad I was able to touch people in a positive light. Sometimes the dark side seems to overshadow anything that beams a little brightness, but I try to live in the crevices filled with light. I've had a lot of people tell me they're thinking twice before having sex, waiting to have children, and going back to school. My wrong decisions may not have always played out in my best interest but they're experiences others can look to. The opportunities I have had along the way to have a positive impact on the world have been amazing. I've met influential people who have helped me to become part of something bigger than myself. For example, Jeff Parshley and Adam Bouska, founders of the NOH8 Campaign, which promotes same sex marriage equality, have created a special silent protest that I participated in.

I'm happier than I've ever been and that's how I want to be seen. I've conquered so much. Sadly, I feel like the Season 4 reunion episode didn't reflect that. The environment was claustrophobic and stuffy. I was frustrated because I felt pressured to meet Jo's girlfriend on stage. I felt like I was being pushed into a corner and my words and feelings were misunderstood.

I did not want a confrontation. It didn't need to change because I didn't care about the relationship. Everyone is entitled to his or her own feelings so why couldn't I just be left alone? I was portrayed as a jealous, psycho ex. I felt I had been manipulated and it annoyed me to the point where I had to get up to leave the set for breathing room. Filming reunion shows is stressful and emotional enough. This was too much for me. I didn't need anyone to play devil's advocate. I already felt enough pressure from this nonexistent relationship I had with Jo's girlfriend. There was too much judgment of my feelings and not enough consideration of the source of those emotions. From the outside it appeared I was just jealous of her for no reason. The show didn't portray her smoking weed or drinking, the way I thought it appeared online. Although Jo denied that she did, that was the reason I held animosity toward her. I just want people to understand that these perceptions of mine were the real reason I had for not liking her or wanting her in Isaac's life.

Believe me, there were opinions galore swirling around. I understand how easy it is to get so invested in people who appear on reality television shows. That's why so many opinions were thrown at me regarding the way I treated Jo's girlfriend or any of my other actions that got people riled up. It was definitely weird to gain all that attention, considering I wasn't used to any at all. Looking back and taking the experience as a whole, I can't view it without mentioning the overwhelming attention.

Maybe I was naïve to not realize how things could skyrocket out of control. I didn't believe I would receive the same sensationalism that some of the other teen mothers had. I thought I would somehow be immune to our culture's obsession with reality TV. I started picking up on certain usernames online who frequently posted about me claiming to know every little detail. It's sort of annoying to have all these facts I didn't even know about myself spilled out from strangers. My favorite color is yellow? No, I believe you might be wrong on that. How do I know? Well, I kind of know Kail.

Even the people who think they know me better than I know myself aren't as bad as the ones who creep on me in public. I don't mind if someone wants a picture or wants to say hi. I'm okay with being approached as long as it's done in a polite manner. It's really sweet and flattering when I hear I've done something that has changed a person's thought process. I really do enjoy meeting new people, but I don't like to see stalker-like photos of me surfacing on the Internet. There's a super stealth shot that exists of me chowing down at Applebee's. (Oh, yeah.Half price appetizers! Who doesn't get excited for that?) As much as I love discounted food, I don't want to see a picture of me with a mouthful of potato or something. I'm not a spectacle.

If anything, I'm an example. I'm a bad example. *Kids, don't be like me!* The reason I've owned up to my mistakes so earnestly in public is to teach others a lesson. Don't follow in my footsteps. I'm not saying I'm some incredible role model. I'm telling you to learn from the hardships others are so willing to give you. There's nothing easy about being a young mother. We are not financially set at all. MTV didn't set us up with never ending bank accounts or blank checks. They gave us airtime and, yes, with my paycheck I was able to pay bills and get a leg up, but I'm not a millionaire or even close to it.

I hope my journey through the trials and tribulations of motherhood have been an inspiration to others who may be facing similar problems. Showing the harsh realities on television to viewers was even more difficult in the long run. I hope somewhere along the way I have inspired someone to make better decisions. That's all I can really ask for.

Ultimately, there's only one message that really matters: always practice safe sex. Use condoms. Use multiple forms of birth control. Wait to have sex. Why rush into something you're probably not ready for? Sex is for adults. As much as sex is glorified in our culture through music and all forms of media, it's not everything. I had to learn this the wrong way. I wish I hadn't looked for love in the wrong places. I wish everything could be different. But wishing doesn't get you anywhere.

Unfortunately, there are no second chances. The consequences of my mistakes were shown on television and my reactions, good and bad, were broadcast for the entire world to see and judge. Would I change anything? If there were second chances, of course I would alter certain aspects of the television experience and possibly the way I handled things. But I regret nothing. Life is all about learning. Since I can't change the past, I'll tightly grasp onto the lessons for the future.

21

CHOCOLATE WASTED

Jaeger bombs, margarita pitchers, random make-out partners, and flavored vodka are all typical twenty-first birthday party favors. *Shots! Shots! Shots!* I can already see the douchey Jersey fists pumping in the air. I guess I could have found a club to party and get hammered at. I could have made bad decisions with my friends, but I have a number of good reasons why I didn't. I don't have anything against drinking, just the repercussions of how the user deals with the substance. Can you blame me, though? I've seen what can happen when you're addicted to alcohol. I am afraid the same addiction runs through my blood.

It was so nice to see Chelsea's birthday celebration for her twenty-first. She looked happy on television and I'm glad MTV was able to capture a normal day in a teen mom's life.

Behind the scenes.

I'm also relieved that, due to the fact that we weren't signed on for another season at that point, they weren't able to film my big milestone birthday. Actually there wasn't much to see. I hung out in my pajamas all night at home. A little Ben and Jerry's and old TV reruns were as thrilling as it got for me on the big two-one. I had a special birthday dinner but that was the extent of my wild night out.

It's hard to say if circumstances had been different, would I have gone out and partied hard. Maybe a couple girly cocktails here and there but I highly doubt I would have gotten trashed and tried to dance on the bar *Coyote Ugly* style. I'm more of a homebody. As a mom, it's a rarity to get a relaxing night at home on the couch. I wouldn't trade that peace for a rowdy, loud time at a bar for anything.

I don't know if that part of me will ever change. I can legally drink now whenever I please. I can go buy a six-pack of beer or a bottle of wine from the liquor store. I can walk into a bar and order whatever I want, but the new freedom doesn't really appeal to me all that much. Plus, there's no age limit to when you can stop doing these things. I have my entire life to drink. Why rush it?

Once Javi and I move to the military base, I know I won't be going out much either. Primarily, my obligations are to my family. I've got them to look after. Plus, I don't know if I'll feel comfortable with having a stranger watch Isaac. Leaving your children with a babysitter is handing over trust to another person to be their protector and caregiver. Once we move, I won't know anyone well enough to entrust with that huge responsibility. When and if the opportunity comes my way, I'll probably take it. I've just never been so crazy about the drinking experience or more specifically, the bar scene. Growing up with a mother who worked as a bartender and who spent a lot of her time hanging out at them, makes the scene even less appealing to me.That's where I fall short in relating to people my age. As a young person in her early twenties, bars and clubs are where I'm supposed to be hanging out, but for me being a mother comes before partying. It's unfortunate because I do consider myself to be a social person.

On the other hand, hanging out and keeping friendships afloat hasn't been my forte either. I've lost a ton of people along the way, but I've also gained friendships around the country. It's fun to know people in different states, but it means fewer friends you can call on to hang out with over the weekend. The struggle to maintain friendships is even more of a challenge now that I am a young adult and living a fast-paced, grown up life. Living in two different worlds has become a barrier between myself and everyone else my age. My plans for a Friday night typically consists of a movie and some dinner, while for most people my age the normal idea is to go out, buy a couple of mixed drinks, and mingle with members of the opposite sex. Or the same sex. Whatever floats your boat.

I totally understand why that's typical. Most young adults are single and not looking for anything serious. There are some young moms out there who want the chance to have their party time, too. Of course, I get why mothers want to go out, let loose, and have fun. It's just that I can't do that spontaneously, or even sometimes when it's planned out. Most mothers get to have their sunshine time to party and go wild. But when you're a teen mom, you're forced to grow up and give up many things in life that you otherwise would have had.

I never went through a period of denial and destruction. From the moment Isaac became a part of me, I realized it was time to grow up. There wasn't anything so terrible about that. My son means the world to me, so I'm okay with the sacrifices I have to make. My friends probably find the sacrifices admirable, but it doesn't mean they fully understand how that affects my social life. Having a son changes the way a young adult functions.

Jo does take Isaac for weekends and such, so I do get to shop and catch up with my friends. I'm not in complete isolation or close to it. On top of having a child, I've taken my relationship with Javi to a level of commitment most people my age aren't ready for. Marriage seriously impacts how you go about your daily life. My decisions aren't only based upon my needs and Isaac's. Javi and I compromise and function as a single unit.

Being married at a young age wasn't much of a question considering I was already doing adult things. It just made perfect sense. When you've aged a decade but your skin doesn't show it, you're going to find yourself living in a different way. I'd rather go with nature then fight against it. Marriage has provided me with stability. It's a dynamic that's difficult to understand unless you're part of it. As my old friends are out picking up guys and having fun, I've become less interesting to them. They just don't come around anymore.

If the opportunity arises to hang out, my current friends are either married or have children. We're on the same level of thinking and our lives are similarly structured. I still like my friends that aren't parents or married, but it's hard to relate to them anymore. Going out is at the forefront of young adulthood. I can't be part of that so it's taken a toll on my social life.The worst part is not having the person I want to be around. With Javi in tech school, it's even harder to want to be having fun. He's the one I want to be out and about with.

I guess what I've really been trying to take a stab at explaining is how fickle and phony friends can sometimes be. Friends are so hard to come by, let alone loyal, good ones. There always seems to be some extra motive or hidden personality trait that eventually rises to the surface. I've met people who I thought were cool because they were so nonchalant and casual. They acted like they didn't care that I was on TV, then a week or two later I'll find out that it's the exact opposite. Question after comment, it becomes clear that all they care about is the show. I usually end a conversation as soon as a "friend" brings up anything that involves *Teen Mom 2*. Why? I'm more than "the girl from *Teen Mom 2*." I'm more than a girl who got pregnant and ended up on MTV.

My castmates are the only ones who can fully appreciate how it's such a drag to be known like that. We are all regular people who don't want to be treated like some gimmick. I'm grateful to have had these girls in my life. Watching the show, it's pretty obvious all of us represent something different. That we can all surely agree on. Jenelle, Chelsea, and Leah all became part of my life in some crazy twist of fate. I don't know if we'll be friends for a little while or forever. I guess the test of the time will be the deciding factor.

Gauging it so far, I believe Leah and I will probably be friends forever. We've only been growing closer and closer since the show began. Chelsea and I catch up once in a while via texts. As for Jenelle, I've done my best to encourage her and help her in any way I can. I wish her only the best and I hope she truly gets better. Jenelle is capable of doing great things. She's a strong girl.

As we try to keep each other informed of the events in our lives, small or large, we'll always be tied together. It's nice to know this whole, wild journey was collectively shared between us, even though we only seldom saw one another. For us, filming *Teen Mom 2* was just a storytelling experience that became such an amazing opportunity to broadcast an important message to young girls.

22

BABY IN HER BELLY

I was pregnant again. Err . . . surprise? Well, it should have been! The gossip sites shouldn't be applauded for snooping in. I had wanted to proudly announce my pregnancy myself, in my own time. I was one hundred percent ecstatically brimming with new life. This time around I was very, very excited! The birth of a baby is a blessing, and the blessing bestowed upon my family was nothing but pure joy.

We attempted to keep the beautiful miracle a secret as long as possible. I delayed the announcement as long as I could in order to keep the media from swooping in. The pregnancy was the main reason I didn't have even one drink on my birthday or why relating to my childless friends was becoming even harder. Being married and pregnant with my second child pushed me even further into an adult lifestyle, rather than the college one I would probably have otherwise been leading.

In February of 2013, I had gone down to Texas for Javi's graduation. Even though he couldn't leave base on Valentine's Day, once we were able to have time alone, we consummated cupid's holiday in a very loving fashion, the way sex is supposed to be. (It was a day later but it's never too late to show your love!) Nothing had been planned. Javi and I had wanted to have children together down the line, but we had never set an exact time frame. Nevertheless, we weren't opposed to the idea.

It wasn't long before the signs started adding up. I had been craving avocado and guacamole like crazy. I thought it was just a food craze I was going through. You know, the little obsessive stages where you'll love a certain food for weeks. I didn't necessarily link food phases to being pregnant, but my friend Toni, a mother of three, told me I should probably check into it.She wasn't so convinced my cravings were normal. My period was due the following week, so I wasn't completely sure if this was pregnancy cravings just yet, but I took her advice and grabbed a pregnancy test. Sure enough, within thirty seconds the stick turned positive.

Since this was a happy pregnancy, I really wanted to share the good news with Javi in person. I wanted to wait until he was home from training to break the great news. But in the end, I really couldn't contain myself, so I took to Skype with Isaac. His beaming face reminded me of all the reasons why I wanted to form a bigger family for him. I knew he was going to break into a fit of joy.

"Mommy has a baby in her belly," Isaac announced.

Javi immediately cried. In between bouts of blissful tears, he managed to express his emotions. He was just as pleased as I was. It was easily one of the best moments ever. There was no questioning *how* we would do this. There were no questions regarding anything. I didn't have to wonder if Javi would stick around. I didn't have to go through all of the worry this time around. The man who loved Isaac so much was going to give him a sibling. We were forming our family.

The easy part was over. The pregnancy was just beginning. Since every pregnancy is different, I didn't know what to expect for round two. The first ten weeks were nearly unbearable. The fatigue and nausea kept me confined to my bed for a majority of the day. Not having Javi around made it tougher. I didn't have someone to share the happy moments with or to turn to for support. Obviously, no situation is totally ideal, but I wish Javi could have been around for the early stages.

I also wished I was in better shape. At five months, I was already twenty-five pounds heavier than I was when I was at that point in my pregnancy with Isaac. In that sense, I knew the weight loss and keeping myself on track would be harder post pregnancy. But overall, my main focus was on maintaining a healthy body for my baby. Fat or thin was no longer the image I concentrated on. Whatever healthy looked like, that's what I wanted.

My finances and living situation were a hundred times more stable than when I was pregnant with Isaac. Without the anxiety, I now had real choices in how I wanted the pregnancy and birth to go. I wanted to take advantage of the fact that I had time to look into options. I was interested in water birthing and birthing centers in the area. I decided this time I would use cloth diapers to go the reusable route and be environmentally friendly. They're also more economical. The cost of disposable diapers adds up fast since you go through them like water.

But, the idea I became quickly obsessed with was dehydrating the placenta to encapsulate and eventually ingest. That disgusting, slimy, organ is controversial, considering it doesn't always work for everyone, but I read that there are many potential benefits, such as increased milk production and energy. It also can help balance hormones and replenish iron levels. I decided to test it out myself to see if I could feel the difference. It's totally natural! And cannibalism was the farthest topic from my mind.

I kept one decision from Isaac's birth. Javi and I talked about names, but I remained firm on my decision to not find out the gender until birth. Gender doesn't matter. Healthy matters. I wanted to have a fully developed, healthy baby. You can't ask for anything more. That didn't stop Javi and me from being creative, though. All of our ideas for names were very unique. There was no Thatcher or Rain to represent the hippie category, but we definitely wanted to beat out Chris Martin. Maybe Apple or Moses? The latter would have been a little ironic on my part, considering my atheism.

23

MILSO LIFE

On top of taking care of a toddler and being pregnant with my second child, I piled more onto my plate by working as a dental assistant. I had to continue to pursue a career and, for now, this was how I had chosen to pay the bills. I enjoyed what I was doing for the time being. There's a sense of pride to utilizing your training and schooling to pave your own way. Did I believe being a dental assistant was my true calling? No. It felt like a bridge. Eventually I would cross over into something I was much more passionate about. I just needed to figure out what that would be.

It was hard to be planning to return to school or to figure out what my career would be, when our future was dependent on where Javi would be stationed first. My stomach nearly dropped out of my body once we received the announcement in early spring of 2013. We were moving to . . . Kansas. *Kansas?* Out of all the possibilities, I wasn't expecting to be placed in the middle of nowhere. Obviously, you have to be flexible and prepared to be living far from home, but I had assumed that "far from home" would be someplace like Texas, California, or Florida. I never thought Kansas.

My initial reaction was tears. I bawled my eyes out for a while as the list of drastic changes grew in my head. I had already changed so much to fit my surroundings, but this was moving to the next extreme. As much as I had zoomed around northeastern Pennsylvania, I'd never been anywhere else for too long. For the first time in my entire life, I'd be moving out of state.

The shock only held for a little bit. I pulled myself together and began making plans for our new life. I had a friend out in Kansas who graciously helped Javi and me search for a house, but more importantly she provided a sense of stability. I wouldn't be totally alone in terms of friendship. House hunting with help wasn't as challenging as the other looming problem. I immediately filed a petition with my lawyer in order to make it possible for Isaac to move to Kansas with me. I was afraid of a big showdown for custody, and by no means was I going to purposely poke the bear. I crossed my fingers for smooth sailing with custody negotiations.

A month passed by quickly without much progress. I was starting to panic as it looked like Javi and I would have to live apart until custody could be properly arranged. Sadly, that was looking at it positively. Three days before Javi was due to report in Kansas, I was working on a client and noticed he was blowing up my phone up. I was worried there was something wrong, but I couldn't answer. Javi drove down to my office to dispatch the news in person. His orders had been diverted from Kansas to Delaware. I cried for joy among the dental tools. We were now moving to Dover, Delaware, a mere two hours from home. *Goodbye Dorothy and Toto. We're not in Kansas anymore.*

I was so grateful for the sudden shift in plans. Not everyone is gifted a short move. And as a military wife, it is my duty to be supportive and flexible to meet the tough lifestyle. Moving around was a part of my childhood, so changing military bases every so often wouldn't feel too unfamiliar. Even as I kept a positive attitude, I was still a little afraid to leave my chosen family behind. There would be no more texting them to meet up in a few minutes.

Immediately, Javi moved down to Dover but since it was so close we were able to see each other on weekends, another benefit of the drivable distance to Pennsylvania. There would be no vicious court battle for custody. I was really starting to relax into the idea of Delaware as we planned our future. The following months were dedicated to finding a house, a permanent residence, in our new town.

Dover isn't the most happening place in the world, but to me it was the most exciting location ever. I was so happy to have the three most important people in the world with me to begin the journey. Javi, Isaac, and the baby are my world. This was a chance for us to be a whole family. The prospects are so bright. Javi has kicked off a new life, flourishing with opportunities for all of us. Isaac will be able to grow up having so much more than I ever did. The baby will have an absolutely clean slate, never having been included in the Pennsylvania part of my life. There will be no more getting through things and just scraping by. Adjusting to a new place takes time, but I would have plenty to keep me busy. Another incentive was finally making friends with others in my situation. Getting to know some other MilSo (Military Significant Others) would definitely help the transition.

24

MOVING ON OUT

Delaware called loudly for our attention. Under the extreme stress of such a big move, I began gathering every hectic part of our lives—prioritizing and crossing the crazy off the list. I tackled the tedious process of labeling boxes and tossing out unnecessary items. The list of to dos weighed me down and the hot summer sun took a toll on my pregnant body. I couldn't wait to be living under one roof with my family instead of the hodgepodge lifestyle we currently had of Javi living in a fluorescent-lit hotel and me a state away.

The separation was wasn't even the worst part. I had been living out of boxes for months to try and hold out on fully moving. It wasn't hesitation. I was hoping we'd score a court date soon so Jo and I could work out a more feasible custody agreement, one where we weren't driving back and forth so much. I felt like the judge wouldn't be likely to grant us anything if we'd already moved. Javi thought I wasn't moving because I wanted to keep working at my job, but really I was just stalling. I was worrying myself to death each day, picking through the mail, hoping to come across good news. If Javi and I were forced to keep living apart, how would our marriage work? It wouldn't.

Finally, I got the letter for which I had been so anxiously waiting. October. It would be that long before we could see the judge for a pretrial hearing. October was still months away, so I decided, now that we had at least received a court date, it was time to join my husband and reunite my little family. In August, I packed up the last of my belongings and headed south to fully settle into our new home. The completeness I felt leaving the empty house in Pennsylvania signaled I was close to closure and a fresh beginning. I truly believed that the moment I stood in front of my new home in Delaware. The immeasurable excitement took control of my body as I gazed at the oversized front lawn, imagining Isaac running around in the even bigger backyard. The new space provided a real start for our family. I couldn't believe this modest, two-story home, complete with trees and shrubbery, was mine. The white picket fence didn't come included, thankfully—that would have been just a tad too traditional for me.

It didn't take long to feel comfortable in our new home. Painting the generic white walls and placing photos and personal touches around created a sense of warmth. Of course our new home didn't replace the family and friends we were missing, but I knew it was going to take some time to get used to the idea of not being able to see them on a moment's notice. My main priority was Isaac. I needed to make sure we helped him assimilate to his new environment. He had already moved around so much, but this was a much more permanent situation and I wanted to make sure we settled him in properly.

We signed up Isaac up for swimming lessons on Tuesdays to provide a sense of structure and normalcy. My dream of becoming a soccer mom (minus the minivan) flourished. Saturdays out on the green grass, where Javi shared his love of soccer with Isaac, balanced some quality family time into the equation. The only complication in this new schedule for us all was the weekly two-hour drive back to Pennsylvania to bring Isaac to Jo, especially since my belly being in oversize mode prevented me from doing it myself.

If I hadn't been pregnant, adjusting to our new life in Delaware wouldn't have been so challenging. That's life, though. There will be a calm before the storm and then a full-fledged hurricane at the worst of times. This hurricane happened to come barreling down on us at the busiest moment imaginable. Moving, planning a wedding, preparing for a baby, dealing with pregnancy sickness, and uprooting a toddler all meshed into a cyclone of worry and anxiety. It was worth it once the moving was over, but as anyone who has ever moved can tell you, it can be one of the most stressful events a person can go through.

Weddings fall into that category, too. The planning, especially the financial aspect, was such a heavy weight on my shoulders. Javi couldn't help much with the planning, which was completely fine, but doing it alone felt like every little accomplishment I checked off the list barely made a dent. I had started to plan the wedding before I got pregnant. This became problematic as I had already picked out my dress and had envisioned myself being thin and fit as I walked down the aisle. Now I would be sporting a large bump, which meant I would have to get my dress altered or find a new one altogether. On top of that, finances were kicking the crap out of Javi and me. Leading up to Delaware, he was living in a hotel and I was still paying rent and utilities. While the additional financial strain of planning a wedding was an expected challenge, the fun parts like planning the bachelorette party were proving to be difficult as well. Coordinating an outing for my bridesmaid party was starting to feel like the equivalent of making down payments.

My bridesmaids came from different circles, so uniting these pieces of my life as a surprise was too difficult for my maid of honor. Christina Pietrobon, aka Peach, had gone to high school with Javi and, even though we only became close while he was at basic military training, it only seemed natural for her to fit the role of being my right hand in the wedding. Aria was my original MOH but since we had not been on good terms for the past eight months, I had already chosen Peach. Instead Aria was a bridesmaid and having her back in my life at such a significant moment completed the circle of our friendship. Kimberley Beall, Genesis Cordova (Javi's cousin), Lidia Marroquin (Javi's sister), and Alecia Aungst were my other bridesmaids. It felt right to have Javi's family be part of my bridal party. After all, in many ways, it wasn't just Javi I was marrying.

Peach attempted to surprise me with a fun mini road trip for the bachelorette party. Picture glorious mountains and really getting away from the annoyances in your daily routine, and that's where we were headed. Her efforts were valiant, however, due to conflicting schedules, there were only four of us heading up to Mount Airy, a little casino up in the Poconos. The scenic view from the casino of the clear water and grassy pastures was nice enough, but we had another view in mind. Thunder From Down Under was our destination for the evening. In a nutshell, it's a bunch of bronzed, half-naked Australian men prancing around, gyrating, and essentially stripping. Javi's bachelor party went the manly route—football, beer, and a strip club. From what I know, they had a great time. How can you go wrong with dollar bills and scantily clad women?

These milestones are more meaningful for me considering I had missed so many along the way. That's why it was so important to me that Javi and I have a celebration of our marriage. It was a public way of solidifying what we have. Marriage brought the three of us together and molded us into a family. Even though my take on marriage is simple and nothing too far out of the box, I wasn't about to be boring or too traditional either.

25

STATE OF LOVE AND TRUST

SEPTEMBER 21, 2013

The dress hugged my hips and flowed down like waves rolling onto the shore. The lump in my throat wasn't from nerves. It was from pure excitement. The day had finally arrived where wearing the white lace dress with subtle floral lining didn't revolve around a dress up game or fantasizing about marriage. This was the real deal here.

The anxiety I felt during the first few hours of preparing myself for a smooth ride down the aisle had nothing to do with cold feet. In fact, my feet were incredibly warm and ready for the walk down the aisle to my two favorite people on this earth. The fast pumping of my blood and heart palpitations had more to do with the crazy energy around me. My wedding party bounced around me effortlessly, pushing a pin in my hair or beating a barely perceptible wrinkle out of my dress. There were at least twenty heads swimming around my room.

The camera crew's sincere effort to remain inconspicuous failed. Since this wasn't a regular day of shooting, there was so much more to the production. Think extra hands, lights, large HD cameras, and total chaos. On top of transforming my wedding venue into something resembling a movie studio set, there was a new director who had to have been feeling the pressure. The director wanted me to stick to a certain schedule, but my mind wasn't cemented to time blocks and place markers. I wanted to really enjoy the moment and soak in every detail of the day.

While the MTV crew was trying to do their job, I positioned myself in one frame of mind: go with the flow, not a schedule. I had already cooperated by allowing MTV to hire my photographer in order to ensure I had no ability to sell my wedding day photos. These little things that may have killed someone else's wedding plans didn't affect me. The real reason behind a more extravagant celebration of our marriage was to show the way we truly feel about each other in front of our friends and family. Our ups and down have been televised for everyone to witness. Now, we wanted to have the opportunity to share in a positive day of love and happiness. The other important reason was to solidify our family and our love. Any anxiety I felt throughout the day disappeared once I saw Javi and Isaac waiting for me.

Sadly, many members of my own family were not present in the flesh on my big day. My two cousins, Jen and Candy, unfortunately couldn't make it. They were originally supposed to accompany me down the aisle, but due to unforeseen circumstances plans had to be changed. Carly and Kaylie and my Aunt Beth were present, though, and my mom's best friend was there, too. It was important to me for her to be present. She was family.

The Camden Aquarium in New Jersey magically set the scene with its stunningly beautiful environment. The whirlwind of emotions and thoughts halted as I saw Javi waiting for me and beaming so brightly. My eyes darted and stuck to my little boy. I hadn't seen him all day and the separation had brought up emotions I wasn't prepared for. I felt such a strong tug at my heart. I loved him so much. Isaac's tux was complete with a grey dress coat and purple vest. My little man looked dapper among the many groomsmen. He is my everything and will be forever. That's why Isaac escorted me down the aisle to my husband.

His small hand engulfed in mine reminded me we were in this together. My eyes couldn't contain the tears any longer. I was so genuinely happy. Isaac couldn't equate bawling and joy together, but his confusion subsided as we met Javi at the front of the ceremony. His hands met mine, warming up my cold nerves. Isaac joined us and held our hands. "You listen to her," he said to us, referring to the Justice of the Peace. Javi and I grinned at how adorable, yet demanding he was. Although small in stature, Isaac's presence was made up for in personality. His little comments here and there put an even wider smile on my face. Isaac stood by my side throughout the ceremony. It's where he belonged because he is my heart and soul.

We ended the ceremony with our own personal touch. Javi, Isaac, and I each poured various colored sand into one container. As the colors mixed, our unity was symbolized. Together, we were now officially one. I didn't see this day as a celebration solely for Javi and me. It was for all of us. Every few minutes I received a compliment on the venue and the food. I wanted the night to be enjoyable for everyone, not just myself. Through all the tribulations, the wedding had come together as a night to remember. I really felt like a land mermaid, surrounded by fish while reaping the perks of a human life.

I had Isaac by my side for the majority of the night. I had expected him to grow bored or maybe become a little sleepy, but he never got cranky, cried, or did anything negative. He was the definition of perfection. Javi was perfect too, of course.

"We should get married again." Isaac's excited voice reminded me of the beautiful future we would have together. "It was SO fun!"

"1,000 Years" by Christina Perri played over and over in my head as the image of Javi and me sharing our first dance together collided with the sound.

♦

Even though everything had unfolded perfectly, I had worried there was a chance the night could go astray. During the planning and leading up to the ceremony I had one concern that I could not shake. Alcohol has a way of turning

Javi and Isaac.

OPPOSITE: Isaac learning to swim. ABOVE: Swimming with Isaac at a friend's house in Dover, PA.

a celebration into a disaster. Javi's family and some of our friends like to drink socially, so I felt obliged to provide a cocktail hour and fully stocked bar. This was a party after all and I knew that I shouldn't generalize my experiences and apply them to every guest. Hoping for some non-slurring company, I had tried to get my bridesmaids to promise me they wouldn't drink, but none of them really made any blood oaths to abstain.

Naturally I felt a little guarded, but to my complete surprise and relief not one single guest drank to the point where it upset me. I was able to enjoy dancing and speaking with the people who had chosen to drink. This was so important to me and I was genuinely pleased everyone held to my expectations.

I had assumed all drunk people transform into monsters of destruction. The uncontrollable stupidity of those who can't walk a straight line disgusts me, but more than that it frightens me. What I have finally come to realize is that alcoholics are the extreme. I have a negative association with drinking and it is an unhealthy and extremely general way to think about it. I've changed though. I've learned. It's okay to drink socially, in moderation, or to kick back and have a beer after a long day. It's just about being responsible and not acting like a complete idiot. I was put in my place even more at my wedding, as a healthy middle ground was found by all. Out of all my wedding-related worries, I was shocked at how well this minor part had gone.

♦

The celebration was over and after a few days the rush of pure joy was running a little thin. I wasn't prepared for post-wedding blues. The high adrenaline and delight of the day naturally had to dwindle down, but I had no idea there was something other than that lurking in my head. The fact of the matter is my mother and father were not present at my wedding. Most people would be sad to hear that or to imagine being in a similar situation. At the time, I didn't care. I had Isaac and Javi. What more could I ask for, right? I honestly had no idea that I had any feelings of regret.

At the next day of shooting, MTV asked me to do some pickups—a little self-reflecting on camera. This impressed upon me some feelings of wedding nostalgia and forced me to look inward. I had no choice but to let my head wander over the ugly fact that my parents were missing at one of the biggest days of my life. The more I did so, the more infuriated I became with my mother. I was pissed because I felt she had never pulled it together for me. Being a mother myself, I will never understand what could be more important than your child. Even though I do understand that addiction changes your perception of what's important, the anger and hurt hasn't disappeared as quickly as I would have liked. I hadn't anticipated crying on camera because I hadn't allowed myself to feel any emotion about the lack of blood-related family at the wedding.

It was my choice not to extend an invitation. I had decided I would rather not stick my neck out and put them in a position to let me down. I felt like neither of my parents had ever been around when I truly needed them. I thought giving them the opportunity to appear as if we had a normal relationship would have been a mistake on my part. My mom did call me as I was getting ready, but I didn't answer. She probably wanted to come, but I wasn't changing my decision. In that sense it must seem like I put myself in a position to be miserable and that I never gave her a chance. I just didn't

Dancing with Isaac at the wedding.

want her to appear like supermom during one of the most joyous and memorable moments of my life. Since I didn't believe she had been there for me during all of the terrible times, why would I allow her to sneak back into my life now?

As for Raymond, I feel that he has been even less of a parent to me. My mom was more of a dad to me than he ever was. I am at peace with my father not being there. He has never really been in my life, so I had no need to have him at my wedding.

Their absence didn't go unnoticed. I was sure our family and friends were aware of the situation. Javi had even tried to convince me to change my mind. His argument was valid. I did only have one mother and this was my huge wedding day. I got that he was trying to help me avoid feeling regret down the road, but my pride intervened. I wanted to remain steadfast on my decision. Besides, Javi has a huge, loving family and their genuine support and love was the icing on the cake that day. I know they will always be there for me.

26

LITTLE LINCOLN

"I'm gonna go into labor tonight," I announced mid-football game.

The loud cheers dulled down in the freezing air as I held onto my stomach and read the expressions on everyone's faces. Javi and our two new friends, Chris and Wendy, stared back blankly. How did I know? The frigid air may have been sending slight shivers down my spine, but there was another unsettling feeling lurking. It was the same feeling I had the night before I gave birth to Isaac. My baby would be arriving in this world soon.

I was sort of upset the pregnancy was almost over. The beauty of carrying a child had been overshadowed by all of the constant stress of the past few months. I felt like I hadn't had time to make a connection with the baby because I had been so preoccupied with trying to balance too many things—the move, custody issues over Isaac, planning a wedding. The nine months had swept by without hesitation or warning and now the major anxiety of it all was crashing down on me.

At midnight the cramping began. The signs were all the same. I told Javi I was in labor, but he dismissed it. He knew how overly worried I could be so he said I should go to sleep. Three hours later, I woke Javi up. The cramps were so strong I could no longer sleep. This was it.

Javi called and left a message for my doctor. I had been freaking out over my doctor of choice being present for the birth, even though he had promised to be available for whenever I went into labor. As Javi called the standby MTV camera girl, I crossed my fingers that my doctor would arrive at the hospital shortly after us. Isaac was still sound asleep in his bed, so I was more than grateful Javi's mother had been staying with us in case this sort of emergency occurred. At four in the morning, Javi and I arrived at Kent General Hospital in Dover. We had gotten there just in time, as my contractions were now five minutes apart.

Since cameras weren't allowed in the hospital, someone from the MTV crew handed Javi a flip camera and insisted he grab some footage. He filmed what we were comfortable with, which didn't include the actual labor. It was very stretched out, two hours longer than Isaac's fourteen-hour birth. Thankfully, I was nowhere near as irritable as I was then.

The scene in my hospital room was the complete opposite this time. It wasn't overcrowded or noisy. Javi was my only support and he proved to be better than a boatload of people encouraging me to push. Javi sat by my side and did his best to calm me down. I didn't yell once or become annoyed with him at all through the slow hours leading up to the delivery.

Even though I had looked into various options, I didn't have a specific birth plan. I only wanted pain meds if I asked for them in the moment. Finally, the doctor (who thankfully had arrived without a hitch) told me I was ready to push. Javi's face turned pale. He looked down for a moment and then back up at me.

"I think I'm going to pass out," he said quietly.

Three pushes later I had a new baby and (thankfully) a fully-conscious husband. I heard Javi say, "It's a boy!" and all the worry and anxiety melted away as the doctor placed my baby in my arms. Lincoln Marshall Marroquin was born on November 16, 2013 at 4:28 p.m. He weighed a healthy eight pounds and six ounces and was twenty-one inches long. He was perfect just like Isaac.

Two days later, we were able to bring Lincoln home to his Pinterest-inspired, gender-neutral bedroom. I had put our dogs at the kennel for a few days to eliminate the insistent barking, so that was one potentially crazy scene out of the way. But, despite all our preparations, bringing a new baby home was chaotic. Even though Isaac had started pre-K in September, we were still adjusting to that schedule. Thankfully Javi had taken ten days off from work so I wouldn't be alone in taking care of two children, yet our house was still a storm of disorder.

Providing undivided attention to two young children in different developmental stages, proved to be an enormous challenge. Nursing Lincoln left me with no free hands to hold Isaac's artwork and proclaim him the next Picasso. Javi adapted to the dynamic. The transition for Isaac was my main

LEFT: Isaac and Lincoln. RIGHT: Isaac, 4, laying with his baby brother Lincoln, 11 weeks old.

concern but Javi put me at ease, ensuring Isaac never felt left out or ignored.

Isaac's enthusiasm was adorable. At first, he seemed a little disinterested, but as time passed he learned to help burp Lincoln and became very engaged. He can't wait until Lincoln is able to talk and play and neither can I. It means so much to me that my boys will be able to experience that special bond shared by siblings. It's something I never had. Isaac will be the best big brother ever and I know he can't wait to teach Lincoln all about *Toy Story*.

I'm excited to see how our lives together will unfold, even if that means going through some stressful custody battles to get there. In October of 2013, we had a pretrial. 2014 will hopefully bring about a healthy agreement between Jo and me. There haven't been any new arrangements yet, so for now Jo gets Isaac Thursday through Sunday every other week and then Thursday into Friday during the alternate week. As much as I can disagree or sometimes not get along with Jo,

I don't see it being like that forever. I want us to have a healthy relationship for Isaac's sake.

Nursing Lincoln before the reunion show, February 2014.

My friend and castmate, Leah, is living proof that you can make one whole family out of two. She and the father of her two children, Corey, have both remarried and Leah loves that his new wife, Miranda, treats their two girls like they were her own. It's beautiful to see Corey and Leah both happily remarried, while maintaining a healthy relationship with one another for their daughters.

That is exactly what I want. Isaac should never feel as though he is the center of the rope that Jo and I are both tugging from opposite ends. We both need to let go, so Isaac has the freedom to move from one side to the other. Hopefully soon, there won't be sides. It'll be a complete circle, our own unique family.

27

THE MERMAID AND DORY

Astrology has depicted my personality and the branches blooming from it. The Pisces symbol's meaning has led me to take an interest in exploring how my astrological sign relates to me. I've also become obsessed with another water symbol, which represents an image I have maintained and has even spawned a parody Twitter account. Oddly enough, it's for my hair and yes, it humors me. Ariel may rock the red, but I have the long blonde hair giving Rapunzel a run for her money. The combination of exaggeratedly long, REAL hair and my astrological sign has branded me as a mythological creature of the sea.

I like to swim deeply and stay away from shallow waters. If I pop up to land, people try to take advantage of my uniqueness and sell me as a story. By now you should have guessed . . . mermaid. I'm a mermaid! Yes, you heard me correctly.

As ridiculous as it may sound, I truly believe in the symbolic nature of these romantic beings.

As for astrology, Pisces are of the sea too. The two fish represent quite a lot about me. I'm past the daily horoscope check. My interest goes much deeper than that. Sometimes the horoscopes are so on point and sometimes they are so very off, but the Pisces sign and what it stands for is what I believe in because it so accurately reflects who I am.

Pisces are afraid of ridicule. Pisces are misfortunate beings. We are open to change. The sign represents how I've adapted to every fishhook thrown in my direction. The Pisces attitude and personality has matched up to mine like a mitten passed down from generation to generation. Like fish in the sea, I've learned to adapt to survive.

As I keep on growing, the next step is more education. I'll be able to pursue a real passion for a career and attend a college. Broadcast journalism has been calling me ever since I began doing voiceovers for MTV and increasingly became more active in creating podcasts. I want to be active, pursue my own reports, and perhaps not shy away from television. We'll see. First, I have to get a Bachelor's degree. I applied to Delaware State and hope to focus on Radio/TV/Film as a major. I want to be in front of the camera because it's not only comfortable but something I want to explore more.

Hope for the future and the current sunshine in my present has brought upon a joyful spirit. I'm the happiest I've ever been. All positive vibes and happiness are here. I'm done living under the scrutiny of people who want to see me fail. I've done my best, even if that doesn't meet everyone's standards.

Sure, I'll still keep the mermaid hair but I'm letting go of the tail and scales. They're too flashy for my taste anyway. I can swim freely without having anyone tugging me back—unless it's Ellen DeGeneres. If Ellen would ever give me the honor to step on her set, I'd follow Dory around the ocean forever.

Just keep swimming!

Isaac and Lincoln.

Acknowledgments

Kailyn Lowry:

Above all, I'd like to first thank the two best little human beings on the planet. Isaac and Lincoln, you both are my heart. Thank you to every single person in my life who has shown complete resilience and stood by me even when I didn't deserve it. To MTV and the Teen Mom crew, I am so appreciative of the opportunity you have bestowed upon me. The blessings and support I have received over the years are due to your patience and kindness toward me. Thank you all so much.

Adrienne Wennner:

My unconventional thanks goes out to my lifelong hero, The Edge. You've always inspired me to reach for perfection within all of my aspirations and to be extraordinary every day. To my two unaware counterparts from the West, Mike McCready and Eddie Vedder, this is for you. Also, thank you to my chosen family for your unconditional support, love, and enthusiasm.